WHO NEEDS A VILLAGE?

IT'S A

Mom Thing

WHO NEEDS A VILLAGE?

IT'S A

Mom

Thing

Helping mothers reclaim their role in raising
the next generation to be successful,
well-adjusted men and women.

DR. ROSEMARY STEIN

978-0692635780

Published by

CALAMO

The Calamo Press

New York City | Washington DC

calamopress.com
Currente-Calamo LLC
2425 17th Street NW, Washington D.C. 20009
244 Fifth Avenue, Ste. D169, New York, NY 10001

This book is dedicated to the many women in my life who at different times, when I needed them most, became a Mom to me. Especially my Aunt Cecilia, who passed away several years ago; my Aunt Peggy; my Mom-friend, Miss Anita; my Canadian mom Marielle; and of course, most of all, my real mom, Cristiana. She never gave up on me when I would have given up on my dreams. Through her perseverance the world will never be quite the same. That is what a Mom does.

I love you, Mom.

TABLE OF CONTENTS

Prologue 9

Introduction 11

Chapter One
Becoming Doctor Rose 17

Chapter Two
Character Building Time................................. 23

Chapter Three
At Last, Our Own Clinic.................................. 29

Chapter Four
Learning First-Hand...................................... 33

Chapter Five
Today's Kids: Overindulged 37

Chapter Six
. . . Overprotected 47

Chapter Seven
. . . And (Definitely) Overstressed 59

Chapter Eight
The Tie That Binds—or That Should 65

Chapter Nine
Meet the Little Tyrant 71

Chapter Ten
Restoring the Mother–Child Bond....................................... 83

Chapter Eleven
The Return of the Little Tyrant.. 91

Chapter Twelve
Nip It in the Bud—Building Tomorrow's Men!.................. 101

Chapter Thirteen
But It's **Never** Too Late.. 107

Chapter Fourteen
The Long Game.. 113

Chapter Fifteen
Give Yourself a Break... 119

Chapter Sixteen
The Healthy Home—How Do We Build It? 125

Chapter Seventeen
Holding Your Ground 141

Chapter Eighteen
Be the Parent You Want Your Child to Be......................... 151

PROLOGUE

This book is dedicated to women everywhere.

*J*think we women have lost our understanding that we are the molders and shapers of society and culture. Whether we have children or not, we still all influence children in some way. Every day, we touch nieces, nephews, schoolchildren, and even other mothers asking us for our advice on raising children. Women are the ones who control how society behaves. If we don't like the way our society treats its women, we must acknowledge that somewhere, at some time, a woman raised her child to treat us poorly. The issue truly is that elemental. More than fifty years ago, mothers were given a new blueprint for raising our children—one that diminished our influence in our children's lives. The unhappy result? Many of the problems we see today in our children and society.

This book will help women to reclaim their role in raising the next generation to be successful, well-adjusted citizens. As I always say in the clinic: "It's a mom thing!"

INTRODUCTION

A few weeks ago, our clinic was turned upside-down by an event that made everyone upset—patients, doctors, and staff alike. In the waiting area, a young man of 15 years was sitting next to his mother. During the fifteen minutes they were waiting, he kept up a constant verbal assault on his mother. He said awful, hurtful things, finally bringing her to tears. He then started to poke her and pretended to punch her over and over. And, of course, this upset the other parents in the waiting room. One by one they came to our front desk to ask permission to physically stop the child; they were concerned for the safety of the mom. The entire clinic came to a halt as everyone searched for a solution to this disturbing problem.

I sent my husband to remove the boy from the waiting area and escort him to an examination room. My husband spent fifteen minutes with the young man describing how men were supposed to act and explaining how the boy's actions fell short of the necessary standard. The boy was doing drugs and planned on dropping out of school; he blamed everything and everyone else for his problems and his failures. Later, the mother related to the pediatrician who was seeing the patient that she was afraid to be alone in her home with her son: She feared for her safety. The boy was out of control around her. His older brother had attempted to stop his actions with no success. Their home situation was so bad that she had been forced to call the police the week before. He was institutionalized for a day because he was out of control.

Since the mother feared not only for her own safety but also that of her other children, the police were called. The scene closed with the boy running away from the clinic and the police giving chase. Mom was left crying in the office waiting area, talking to the other police officer. Her anguish was evident, and no one could console her.

I would like you to travel back in time with me. I have had this clinic and these patients for sixteen years; I have watched them all grow up. I know them and their medical histories like I know my own daughter's. I treat each and every one like family.

I remember this boy when he was just a little child. He was a handsome, charming boy. Everyone at the clinic liked him. He could have a bit of a smart mouth, but we knew he did not mean anything by it. We all ignored those nagging feelings we had. His mother raised her son like many of today's moms raise their children: She doted on the boy. In fact, they were buddies. She often sought his opinion and approval to do certain things or go certain places. Her son was, to her, the most precious child in the world. As I watched her parenting methods, I grew increasingly concerned for Eric's future. His brain was being trained to think that he was the most important person in the world. In today's terms, he was being raised to have very high self-esteem.

The synonyms for self-esteem are *narcissism, egotism,* and *conceit.* These are not character traits that mothers should desire in their children. As Eric was growing up, I spoke with his mother about my concerns. I tried to explain the dangers he faced if he grew up thinking he was the center of his universe. Typically, such boys grow up having disdain for their mothers because they feel the mother is weak and worthless. I did not want this to happen to her son. Unfortunately, like many similar mothers, she was insulted by my concerns. I was not able to talk with her about the subject again. The outcome was the sad story that you have just read.

After more than twenty years of pediatric practice, observing the outcomes of different children, certain patterns have emerged and become clear. When parents raise their child much as this mom raised hers, there will usually be a similar outcome when the child becomes an adult. I implore all moms who read this book: Understand that this is the rule, not the exception. This outcome is independent of race, color, or financial circumstance. It breaks my heart to watch young parents make these mistakes. After all these years, I know the outcome for their child. It is terrible and heart-wrenching. But it doesn't have to be that way.

You are the perfect mom for your child. After spending many years working with parents and children, I know that many moms will find that hard to believe. But it's true. God has chosen you to be the parent of your child. You are the best chance he or she has to succeed in life. No one knows your kid better—and you've got *instinct* on your side.

The problem these days is that there's so much noise out there—so many so-called experts competing for attention, each of them claiming to have all the answers—that this basic fact can get lost.

Your task is to find and reaffirm that maternal instinct and your unique maternal voice for your child. My task is to teach you how to accomplish it. Why is my primary focus on moms when, by every measure, fathers are also important to the future life success of a child? Because despite all the supposed changes in parental roles over the past few decades, certain realities are simply driven by biology—and among them is that nothing is more important to a child's development than a strong mother–child bond. Indeed, in the vast majority of families, dads themselves intuitively understand that it's the woman who is really better equipped by nature to handle the child-rearing, so they reflexively take their cues from the mothers.

So it's important, first of all, to look at why so many moms in today's America have ended up so overwhelmed and unsure—and at how we got to a place where they simply don't *trust* themselves.

The evidence can be found in any bookstore. Walk over to the parenting section, and you're assaulted with row after row of books telling you that you can't do it on your own—that you'll be the "perfect" mom or dad if only you follow their guidance. And what is their advice? Usually, in one form or another, it is that what kids need most is respect and understanding, since they are dealing with all kinds of pressures and anxieties that their moms and dads can't understand; accordingly, kids need to be given more power and control over their own lives.

While this might seem like something new, actually it is anything but. Back in the late eighteenth century, philosopher Jean-Jacques Rousseau gave French intellectuals the same sort of advice. He declared that a child should be given as much freedom as possible—that parents should never even lecture their children. Children were natural beings, he wrote, and would basically educate themselves through the process of living life.

Some might say that the result was the French Revolution.

That's only partly a joke. The fact is, the kinds of advice that many parents are getting these days have inverted the power balance in millions of American homes, and the result is chaos.

In this book, I will talk a lot about parenting *consciously*—about how important it is to understand that the ways we act, as seen in almost every decision we make, can have an impact on our kids. Quite simply, your child's life is bound up in yours, his or her possibilities for success entwined with how you live your life now. All your decisions and actions and attitudes—whether you're bringing yourself up or taking yourself down—your child sees them all and feels them all. It's as if you're a sailboat with a little dinghy tied to the back. The dinghy may be its own little boat, able to float by itself and perhaps even weather a mild storm. But if that sailboat can't handle rough seas and capsizes, then the dinghy will go down with it.

This gets to a concept I will talk about more in the following pages: the long game.

What does it mean to play the long game? Well, first let's very briefly talk about what it *doesn't* mean.

It doesn't mean you have to be perfect, beating yourself up when you fall short. But what it means is, even at those times, being *aware*—understanding the tremendous influence your behavior will have on your child. It also means being, to the extent humanly possible, consistent and clear, as well as consciously establishing a home environment in which there's no question in the child's mind about what the rules and expectations are, nor about who is in charge.

That is the basis of every child's security and proper sense of place in the world. It is the foundation upon which he or she will build a successful life.

Parenting cannot be haphazard; it should be deliberate and thoughtful. And it should start early, at the beginning, when your child is very young—or, even before that, when you're expecting. You have to analyze yourself and your attributes, thinking *Okay—what are my hopes and dreams for my child? What attributes would I like to see in my child? Do I want him or her to be honest? Do I want him or her to be compassionate? What must he or she see in me to help create that?*

Too many parents these days—in fact, most—go into it without any thought or direction at all. Their plan, if you can call it that, is basically *Let's see how this all works out.*

But failing to plan is planning to fail. Would you give a presentation at work completely unprepared? Well, here's the greatest undertaking of your life—raising another human being to be a good citizen and a productive member of society. Why on earth would anyone just wing it?

In the course of the book, I will give examples of children acting out that will be all too familiar to many moms. I will discuss that chaos and how it came about. But my focus will be just as much on the parental behavior that led to it.

This isn't about being perfect parents. None of us is that. We are talking about the most difficult job in the world, as well as the most complicated. What we are talking about is planting the right seeds—building a strong foundation—as early as possible. Sometimes you will have to do it over and over, season after season. But if you do it right—watering, pruning, nourishing—in the end, it *will* bear fruit.

The sooner you start, the better, because over time, the wrong behaviors become established within a child and form the person. Fix it now—or pay for it later. Because kids will go and go and go until they find the boundary. And if they don't find one, then, in the worst-case scenario, prison walls will provide one.

It might not be fun doing what needs to be done, but parenting isn't always about having fun. It's about raising good citizens and bringing glory to the One who gave you this child.

So much of this is really just common sense. We parents need to step forward with wisdom, love, and—yes—discipline. We must remember that the discomfort we might sometimes feel applying these lessons means that we are changing and growing.

Once things are ship-shape, you can have all the fun in the world with your kids and in your role as their parent. What you sow now you shall reap later—a thousandfold!

16

Chapter One

BECOMING DOCTOR ROSE

*L*ike all of us, I am the sum total of my experiences in life. In my case, they involve a quite unusual mix of cultures, as well as exposure to a wide variety of mentors and role models. They have all shaped my philosophy on the right way to raise healthy, motivated, successful children.

Oh, I almost forgot—I, too, have my own (sometimes humbling) experiences as a mom myself that have helped to shape me.

My dad, Diogenes, barely got through fifth grade in the Dominican Republic, growing up under the brutal dictator Rafael Trujillo, while my mom, Cristiana, came from a well-known family of educators. Her father was the superintendent of schools for a large district, and his wife, my grandmother, was the headmistress of a large school in the interior. My great aunt wrote the curriculum for public schools throughout the country. My Aunt Cecilia was an author and founded a large, well-known private school in the capital city, Santo Domingo.

While this contrast in my parents' backgrounds—and how my mother's parents' disapproval of her choice of a husband led to their leaving the Dominican Republic in 1963 for New York—makes for a romantic story, it was a rocky marriage. My father was a heavy drinker throughout my childhood; I was left at home Saturdays with a guy who would sleep half the day away.

It was my mom's influence that truly formed my perspective on life. She arrived in the United States not speaking a word of English and started out at a minimum-wage job in a toy factory. But before long, she signed up for business English at a local community college with a very specific ambition: *I will work on Fifth Avenue one day!* And she did. Four years later, she got a job in the accounting department at Lord and Taylor, on Fifth Avenue.

Quite simply, just by my parents' example—for my father was also a hard worker—I learned a fundamental life lesson, one I now try to impress upon my patients: Successfully making your way in life depends on your own efforts.

Unfortunately, over the past couple of generations, that lesson has increasingly been lost. In fact, I'm told that soon after I was born, my mother had to make a choice. President Johnson had just offered a new social program that paid moms with young kids to stay home—but only if they weren't working. My mom was tempted. She and her sister-in law, my aunt, talked this over after their first day working a new job in a toy factory. My mother, to her credit, decided that she had come to America to work and make her way: She would not sign up for this new program.

Unfortunately, my aunt took the offer and stayed home. After that, she and my three cousins were all on welfare. Through her actions, my aunt taught her family that not working was acceptable—and her three children took that lesson to heart. My three cousins never held a steady job; each ended up with drug problems or engaging in criminal behavior. All three of them died before they reached their fortieth birthday. They left behind eight children who now live with their grandmother—on welfare. And you can trace it all back to that one decision: allowing herself to be taken care of instead of striving for herself.

My mom's expectations for me were always sky-high, and she didn't believe in excuses. Entering kindergarten, I spoke only Spanish, and after the first day, I came home complaining that the teacher had separated me from the only other Spanish-speaking child in the class. Her reaction? "That's good for you! You learn English and you will do well. Never look to speak Spanish at school at all."

By third grade, growing up in Richmond Hill, Queens, I knew I wanted to be a baby doctor—a pediatrician. I don't even know why—maybe because I'd read so much about Helen Keller, and her teacher Annie Sullivan, whom I thought of as not only her teacher but her doctor.

But in 1977, when I was 12 years old, my world turned upside-down. It was the Son of Sam period, and my parents, worried about my safety, decided to move back to the Dominican Republic. Talk about a shock! By now I was a totally American girl.

I spoke Spanish at home, but I didn't write it or read it. In fact, back in the United States, when I was with my loud, Spanish-speaking extended family, I found them embarrassing and completely weird.

So it was a total culture shock: I had to relearn everything. Life was much more regimented than in the United States. Girls my age couldn't go out without a chaperone. I was constantly being told that I didn't have manners, that I had to learn proper etiquette at the table, and all the rest—this after I'd grown up playing in the streets of New York City.

But in a way, as we'll see, this experience—this exposure to a new and different way of raising children—affected the way I approach things now. Life was very different in the Dominican Republic. My mom was starting a school from scratch, and since my dad no longer had a job, he now had seven days to drink. That was the one constant in my life: my dad's drinking. At one point, my mother actually sought counsel for a possible divorce. But the attitude down there, far more than in the United States, was *Uh-unh—that's what you chose. That's your bed; lie in it.*

I helped out at the school my mom was starting, even though I was only a young teenager. It was incredibly challenging, because I was in school myself, of course, but my mom believed I could handle it, and she was right. It was my job to help the first-graders who were struggling to learn to read. Teaching children in those days was extremely regimented. My family of educators would argue for hours about which consonant should be taught first when teaching a child to read. Early education of the child—from kindergarten to third grade—was laid down carefully, brick by brick, to ensure a strong foundation. Each day after I completed my lessons at school, I taught those little kids to read. To make a little money for myself, I also started my own English as a second language program, and I made a dozen kids fluent in English.

When I was 16 years old, my mom decided I needed to be toughened up—and also that I should learn French—so I was matched, through an exchange program, with a family in Quebec. I can still remember my first meeting with my new parents. My

Canadian dad bounded up the stairs of the American Field Service building in Montreal, Canada, and said, in his strong French-Canadian accent, "Hello—I am Jacques Bureau." I replied, "Hello, sir—I am Rosemary Fernandez, your daughter for the year." My life would never be the same.

Another shock. Here I suddenly was in French-speaking classes, and for the first time in my life, I thought I would flunk. Math in French, science in French, *French* in French!

I called my mom, crying about how homesick I was, and got the expected reply: "You're not really sick—just homesick?"

"Yes," I sniffled.

"Well, I *expect* you to be homesick. You're okay; you'll be fine. This call is very expensive—just call me if you're really sick or something bad happens."

There was just no room for self-pity. I had to go ahead and learn French. And, of course, by the time Christmas came around, I was fine. In fact, I ended up crying when I left my wonderful Canadian family and was homesick for Canada. This one year of surrogate parenting by Jacques and his wife Marielle changed the direction of my life. I still make the trip to Canada each year so that they can see their "granddaughter" Hannah as she grows up into a young lady. Eight years ago, on one of those trips, my "father" asked me if Hannah would be allowed to do what I did at 16 years old and become an exchange student. My immediate thought was *No—times and things have changed.* Then, for the first time, I realized that it isn't the times that have changed. What has changed are the parents and the way that we are child rearing. I also realized that I was including myself in this group.

When I got back to the Dominican Republic, I found that my mom had signed me up for pre-med, so I attended medical school there. But I always knew I'd be coming back north to either the United States or Canada—that was my goal. At heart, I was still an American kid.

But coming back to America was a *lot* more challenging than I expected. I was done with medical school at 23 years old, and I had to find my way in an American residency program. I started a sub-internship, and within 12 weeks, it was clear I wouldn't make it through. Quite simply, American med schools were a lot more demanding than those in the Dominican Republic, and I wasn't ready to jump to the next level. I didn't have the terminology base, and I wasn't mature enough to make the decisions required of a first-year resident.

It was *terrible* for my self-confidence, and I had to consider the possibility that maybe I wasn't cut out for this. But I missed the kids, and it would have left a hole in my heart to give up my dream. I knew I had to work it through and up my game.

After a lot of effort, I at last did. But I wasn't ready to hang out my shingle yet.

Chapter Two

CHARACTER BUILDING TIME

M aybe the reason I understand, and sympathize with, those of my patients who come in feeling overwhelmed by life is that in the past, I had my own serious issues with responsibility and follow through. In other words, I learned the hard way.

When you have faults, there are repercussions, and my character weaknesses really showed themselves when I was doing my residency at a hospital in New Jersey—or maybe *my immaturity* would be a better characterization. Whatever the unflattering description, I got a reputation for being a bit of a slacker, too ready to cut corners and maybe not always quite as honest as I should be. And I paid the price. In a very frank conversation at the end of my third year, my program director told me he didn't like me. And he said he didn't even think that I should necessarily graduate from residency.

Then, because he was passive-aggressive, rather than turn in my paperwork to the state licensing board—which would enable me to get accredited and work as a doctor—he simply sat on it.

Meanwhile, I was close to broke and had all kinds of debts. Why? Because I'd been a terrible manager of money. I loved beautiful clothes, only bought name brands, had a nice car, and even spent a lot on highlights for my hair.

So now the chickens had come home to roost. I had to scrounge to find whatever work I could, and I ended up getting three jobs for myself, one of them as an early morning newspaper carrier. Here I am, a doctor, having just graduated from residency, and I'm getting up at 3:30 in the morning to deliver newspapers to pay the rent. And, by the way, I'm terrible at it, the worst newspaper delivery person ever, constantly throwing papers into the wrong yard! Then, for job number two, I'd run over to a YMCA, where from 7:00 to 9:00 a.m. I'd watch over a bunch of kids in before-school daycare. Then I had another little job nannying a baby, after which I'd run back to the YMCA to do an after-school daycare from 5:30 to 6:00 p.m. Meanwhile, the income from those three jobs didn't amount to even a quarter of what I'd been making as a resident—let alone what I should be making as a doctor.

This was a terrible phase of my life. I almost got evicted from my apartment a couple of times, and I had to sell my car. But it finally got the lesson to sink in. I negotiated my debt down significantly—I owed about $15,000 in total but found that most of the major creditors were willing to accept fifty cents on the dollar or even less. Then I called my mom, who lent me the money to pay off what I now owed and get back to even. *That* was a hard phone call to make.

Meanwhile, I'd been regularly calling the office of my former program director at the hospital, trying to get him to send off my file to the board, and pretty soon I struck up a friendship with his assistant. She told me that this is what he did when he didn't like somebody—that maybe I should send him a little note to stroke his ego, because he's a little guy with self-esteem issues. I did, and it went unanswered.

But finally—*finally*—I got word from the assistant that the recommendation had gone out at last, and I'd be getting my interview with the state licensing board. Of course, this was a new worry! I imagined a grand inquisition whose members would be aware of all I'd done wrong and make me pay for it.

And when the interview took place, two or three months later, it was almost as bad as I'd anticipated. They said, in essence, *The record shows that time after time you were tardy and not as responsible as you needed to be. How can you show us you'd be the kind of physician who'll be beneficial to society and to New Jersey?*

I made the only honest case I could, saying *Based on my track record, you're just going to have to take my word for it, because it's true—I don't have a lot to show for myself. But all I'm looking for is a shot to be the best doctor I can be.* I could see then that some of them were sympathetic—which I hoped meant they wouldn't treat me the way I deserved to be treated.

Well, sure enough, a few weeks later, I get a letter from the board with the good news that I had my license—the best news I'd ever had!

The question then became *What next?* And it was complicated by my having just broken up with a boyfriend who went to the same church I did. But in a way, that also made it easier. I decided that if I was really going to start fresh, I should do it in a new place and make the past the past.

Unfortunately, I had only a New Jersey license, but I learned that I could still practice in another state if I worked for the federal government. So I went out and found a position working as a contract officer for the military. Within a week of interviewing, I was on a plane, heading to Fort Campbell, Kentucky.

This was summer 1994, and it was my first job doing what I'd always wanted to do—working as a physician.

The place was pretty isolated, and at the beginning, it sometimes got lonely, but I learned to fill myself up, look for a good church home, and press on.

And it was there, at Fort Campbell, that I met my husband, Dave.

I'd love to say it was love at first sight, but it wasn't. I was delighted to be working there—for me, it was a new lease on life—but here was this guy going around the clinic and moping.

So I said, "What's your problem?"

"It's my birthday."

"So what's so bad about that?"

"I'm 30," he said, like it was the end of the world.

I was 29 years old at the time, about to turn 30—which, if you're from the Dominican Republic and unmarried, really *is* considered a tragedy. "Oh, my goodness," I chided, "you are *so* old. Somebody should just put you out to pasture."

That didn't sit well with him. He looked at me and said, "You're that new doctor, aren't you?"

"I certainly am."

"How long are you going to be here?"

"Obviously long enough to bother you." Famous last words, right?

There were ten or twelve doctors in the clinic, and Dave was an assistant supervisor, in charge of reviewing the pediatricians' charts. At one point, he criticized some of the care I was giving. Naturally, I didn't take very well to that, and I got into it with him—or tried to. But he kept his cool—which, of course, makes a woman who is upset even more upset. Yet I had to respect his demeanor.

Then he got temporarily deployed to Texas to do airborne surgeon training, and he left for three months. And it suddenly hit me: *Hey, I kind of miss that big, mean dude.*

But only as a friend. Because Dave was married at the time, I certainly would never have considered him as a romantic possibility. In fact, his wife would occasionally come in with their son. And I had no reason to know that theirs wasn't a happy marriage.

But when Dave got back from Texas, it's hard not to notice he's walking around looking all depressed. So one night soon after, a group of us from the clinic go out for a beer. He takes a seat next to me—which I don't think anything of, since I figure he just wants a friend to talk to. He tells me that he'll soon be leaving our clinic, since he has been promoted to supervisor of a different clinic in the hospital. And he asks if I could help him shop for some goodbye presents for the secretaries.

What none of us knew was that while he was away, his wife of nine years had been cheating on him with their next-door neighbor. And as if that's not bad enough, she has also maxed out his credit cards, leaving him $20,000 in debt. So he's been in a huge depression trying to deal with all this turmoil in his home—and he has also started divorce proceedings.

All of this comes out on this shopping trip—which is really sort of our first date. And then he pulls an even bigger surprise. He says that in the middle of everything, it hit him that there was one person he wanted to be with the rest of his life.

I looked at him and said, "Oh my goodness—who is that?"

"I'm madly in love with *you!*"

"You're kidding me," I said, genuinely flabbergasted. "I mean, I thought you were acting kind of funny, and now you say it's because of everything going on in your life. But, I mean—*what?*"

That was actually my answer.

It was only an hour's drive back to the base, but it felt a *lot* longer, because I was totally in shock. Here I'd gone out for a shopping trip with this married guy from the clinic, and now he's a soon-to-be-divorced guy whom I *think* has just proposed. And I'm wondering *I'm not a home wrecker, am I?* But, no—obviously not, since this has apparently been going on for months and months and just came to a head. Then, too, I remembered something he had asked me a while earlier—whether I'd ever consider marrying a divorced guy. I thought it just an idle question: Certainly he couldn't mean himself, since he was happily married. So I had answered, very innocently, that I would only under one circumstance, as stipulated in the Bible: if that man's spouse had cheated on him. So I now realized that my answer had made him think *Good, I have a shot!*

And he was probably thinking, too, that he had to act fast, because my year-long contract with the military was expiring soon, and I had already accepted another job in Atlanta.

I'm thinking all of this on that endless, silent ride home. When we get there, it's a little awkward for a moment. But then I kiss him on the cheek and say, "You know, if things were to work out between us, I'd be the luckiest woman in the world."

And one year later, we were married.

Chapter Three

AT LAST,
OUR OWN CLINIC

*B*efore starting my own practice, sixteen years ago, I worked in three other practices, and I took something from each of them.

The first was at Blanchfield Army Hospital (where I met Dave), taking care of children whose parents belonged to the 101st Airborne Division. Military medicine was basically like managed care—long on paperwork and short on immediacy and flexibility. If a patient with pneumonia failed the first line of antibiotics, we'd have to jump though all sorts of hoops before we'd be able to give him or her the next line of antibiotics. This was obviously not good for either doctors or patients. It was there that I had my first up-close experience with the new phenomenon of poor childhood behavior. I was seeing a 6-year-old for an illness, and the child decided that he would not allow himself to be examined. When I tried to examine his ear, he slapped my face—hard. I was so shocked that I held his hand and told him that he should never hurt another person. His mom was so embarrassed that she started to cry. I had never experienced this sort of behavior before. At the time, I remember wondering what could have brought things to such a point. As my career progressed, I was able to put the pieces of the puzzle together to figure out how our society has come so far in the wrong direction.

Next, I worked two years at an urgent care clinic, which was a little better, because more of my patients had insurance or paid for their health care out of their own pocket, requiring them to assume greater personal responsibility for their kids' health. But by the same token, that could be a major downside, because some moms would wait far too long before bringing a child in for treatment. I learned that those parents who did not have to pay for their health care would use the medical facilities for their convenience rather than for the health of their children. This, obviously, did not sit well with me. If, say, someone waited two or three weeks before bringing in a kid with ringworm at 11:30 p.m., I was apt to say, "Listen—as moms, we take care of their health first, and not necessarily as a matter of con-venience." Of course, the mother might get very insulted at that, and I'd soon get a call from patient resources telling me I'd been mean and was judging the mom. In other words, the responsibility and account-ability fell entirely on the doctor. But I believe that when a parent doesn't assume any responsibility for a child's health and welfare, that child will not grow up in an environment leading to the child's best outcome. I had seen this first-hand with my aunt and her family.

After that, I had a small practice of my own, still in Atlanta, under a hospital-managed system. It was great being able to do things my own way. When I'd get a new patient, the parents would come in, and we'd have a little talk so that they understood that they also had responsibility for their kids' health and that they must adhere to certain rules. My parents knew not to call me after hours for routine problems, let alone run to an emergency room, except in an emergency; they understood that they were spending taxpayer money. " Somebody's paying for it," I explained to the mothers in my practice. More important, they understood that taking responsibility for the care and well-being of their child was part of healthy parenting, aimed at producing the best outcome for him or her.

At the same time, in this practice I was obliged to frequently cover for another group with a totally different philosophy, who demanded absolutely no responsibility or accountability from their patients. So when I was on call for them, the phone would never stop ringing, with patients asking questions they could have answered themselves if they'd bothered thinking about their problem for thirty seconds. I'd get calls in the middle of the night: "What dosage of Tylenol should I give him?" *Geez*, I'd think, *read the bottle!*

This wasn't just a matter of annoyance; the real problem was what such an attitude reflected about the callers, because none of it was good for their children. The lives of the children in these homes were chaotic—their parents made no effort and had no organization skills. They waited until the last moment to deal with problems and devoted no forethought to what to do before they hit the wall. Quite simply, they didn't understand their side of growing a child up.

So when my husband Dave and I started our own practice from scratch in 1999, having seen what worked and what didn't, I had a pretty clear idea of what I wanted to do. I wanted a practice that stressed parental accountability and responsibility. And I knew I wanted to spend more time with patients than most pediatricians do, even if that meant less income. We wanted not only to address immediate medical issues but also to teach parents how to parent and how to be responsible, and thus how to ensure the best possible outcomes for their children.

We're a private practice, and we don't take any government grants, so we are able to practice medicine the way it should be practiced. When we're interviewing for new doctors—we have four on staff at any given time—we go through our entire philosophy. Prospects who believe the government is responsible for raising our children are probably not going to be interested in us—nor we in them.

Although probably 70 percent of our patients are lower-income, some pay a co-pay—something between $5 and $25. Although it's not much, it means they have skin in the game. As a result, they tend to value their appointments and their doctor a little more. And when they leave the office, they'll pay another co-pay at the pharmacy. I find that these parents tend to be better at following through with medication and treatment plans.

I don't like to threaten parents when they don't keep important appointments, so we call parents two days before, as well as the morning of, the appointment. My staff will remind the mom of her responsibility to keep the appointment. The fact is, any time you have an investment, you're more responsible: The upshot is that our patients tend to get sick a little bit less. Overall, they and their parents are easier to educate and more responsible.

Most days, at the International Family Clinic, we see anywhere from sixty-five to ninety patients, about half of them Spanish-speaking. In fact, we gave our clinic the name we did because I wanted Hispanic patients to feel welcome. After all this time, we've seen patients grow to adulthood and, in many cases, are now treating former patients' children. This is hugely gratifying, both on a personal basis and because their lives are the clearest evidence of how successful our philosophy has been at helping produce competent and successful adults.

Chapter Four

LEARNING
FIRST-HAND

*T*here is one other fundamental experience that shaped my philosophy as a pediatrician, bringing to it what might be called the element of common sense—becoming a mother myself.

Before that, I was—how should I put this?—pretty dogmatic. Or maybe a better word would be *harsh.*

I'd been practicing five years before Hannah was born, and I had always taught moms that breastfeeding was essential—practically the eleventh commandment—because, without question, mother's milk is easier for the child to digest. I also was firm about *never* leaving an infant alone on a bed, lest he or she fall; and if a mom absolutely had to use formula, she must certainly never microwave it! An organizational freak myself, I'd chastise moms who couldn't do it all perfectly.

Then I had my own child, and everything suddenly became *My goodness, what was I thinking?*

Of all the things God could do to humble me, I couldn't breast-feed! I almost starved my daughter trying. At three weeks, she was skinny as a stick and yellow as a number 2 pencil, because I wasn't producing any breast milk—but still I wouldn't give her formula. I was crying, hormones were setting in, and I convinced myself that if I just drank enough water and did everything else on the list, it would *happen*. Meanwhile, my child was so dehydrated she couldn't stay awake.

Finally Dave walks in and says, "Can you hand me the baby, please?" And he pulled out the bottle: He'd been quietly preparing the formula. That poor thing was as ravenous as a starving child.

And pretty soon there comes a day when I'm on the phone, and there's someone at the door, and I leave my child alone on the bed—so there I go, breaking *that* rule.

Of course, it didn't end there. From two weeks on, our daughter had the most terrible colic, with the sort of endless horrible crying and screaming that could drive a person mad. It was another complaint I'd heard forever—and had never taken all that seriously.

Talk about humbling! I realized how wrong I'd been in judging all those other moms. Truly, this was where theory met reality.

Nor, as time went on, was Hannah a particularly well-behaved child, at least in our eyes. She was defiant and kind of mouthy, and she could be very stubborn, refusing to listen. I found myself yelling a lot and punishing a lot and still not getting her to mind. It wasn't until she was about 10 years old, when I attended a lecture by parenting expert John Rosemond, that it all clicked and I understood how much I'd been doing wrong. I had been reacting to her rather than taking control and acting first.

That realization—the understanding of how wrong I'd been—was as important a lesson as any I've had. It not only made me more accessible and empathetic, but it also reinforced what I'd always known from my own childhood yet, in the hustle and bustle of American life, had too often set aside: Parents must be the center of the home. When you put children in the center of the universe, they get used to it—and they stay there.

My experience with Hannah also taught me that there were at least *some* childcare "experts" out there who really did have answers. For instance, there were Gary Ezzo and Dr. Robert Bucknan, whose book *On Becoming Baby Wise* helped me solve the mystery of getting my infant daughter to sleep through the night, as well as John Rosemond, whom I met at a weekend conference when 10-year-old Hannah had us at our wits' end with her refusal to listen and her other misbehavior. Each of these experts, as you will see, offered important and valuable insights that I have incorporated into my practice.

To be sure, this is far from an exact science, and every child will be different. But there are methods that definitely do work and rules that, if followed, will make the job of parenting immeasurably less stressful and more joyful.

Chapter Five

TODAY'S KIDS: OVERINDULGED . . .

*W*hen I think of the differences in parenting between the United States and the Dominican Republic—and, for that matter, most of the rest of the world—I think back on an episode that made a strong impression on me when I was a young teenager. I had just returned to the Dominican Republic and was doing my bit to help my mother start her school. Since we were on a tight budget, we would sometimes buy things from people who were moving out of the country, and we especially liked Americans, since they'd often sell their children's toys. One day, walking into the playroom of some very wealthy Americans who were about to return to the United States, I discovered a room full of terrific educational toys.

Excitedly, I ran to my mother to tell her to ask the owner if she'd sell some of these great toys.

Seeing this, the woman asked, rather sharply, "Don't you talk for yourself?"

I just looked at her. I spoke much better English than my mom. But I'd also been raised to know that children didn't address adults unprompted.

So that was the first surprise. The second was her reaction. Judging from the toys, her kids couldn't have been more than 5 or 6 years old, but she said, as if it were the most obvious thing in the world, "I don't sell my children's toys—I would have to get their permission."

Stupefied, I looked back at my mom—what is *that*?

So she wouldn't sell them, and we didn't wait around for the kids to come back, so we left. What were we going to do—negotiate with a toddler? Someone who might demand a million dollars for a toy?

What I was left with was: *Whoa, this is crazy! Who's running the show, anyway?*

That was a real insight, because I knew instinctively that not only was something terribly off about giving those kids that kind of power, but also it couldn't be good for them. It wasn't the way to teach them respect, responsibility, or the other habits of a successful life. It could only turn them into pint-sized narcissists.

> Giving kids too much power too early hurts them in the long run, turning them into pint-sized narcissists. Kids need to learn respect, responsibility, and other habits of a successful life.

That was a long time ago, but it's only gotten worse since then. Overindulging kids is the norm today in millions of American households of every income and description. They are little princes and princesses who grow up thinking the entire world revolves around them.

I see examples in the clinic all the time. I had a dad only last week with a 2-year-old who needed medicine for an infection, so I mentioned that they could pick up the prescription at Walmart.

"Walmart!" he exclaimed. "No, we can't do that, because getting Sam out of Walmart is a major production—it will be two hours before we can leave. He won't stop roaming around the store. No—not Walmart." In brief, they had made Walmart the problem, and their solution became to eliminate Walmart from their lives.

> *Parents* have to set the tone, and children have to learn from them. And believe me, they have a lot to learn from you! Too often today, it's the other way around.

"Have you ever tried speaking to him *before* you go to Walmart," I suggested, "so maybe his expectation would be that he's not the one in charge?" The very notion of doing that surprised the father: That had never occurred to him. Nor has it to countless other parents of children young and old. This is how backwards, inside-out, and upside-down things have gotten. Parents no longer take for granted their ability, let alone their responsibility, to set the tone, nor that their children are there to learn *from* them. Too many adults nowadays have their whole lives so wrapped up in their children's worlds that the children's lives become *their* lives.

It is our job as parents to match our children's level of development to what they are able to comprehend and *do for themselves.* This is how they will grow up at the proper pace, becoming competent and successful in life. If you're saying to a child who is 2 or 3 years old *you choose* what food to eat or what clothes to wear, what you're telling him is that he is able to do something that he is not equipped to do. Obviously, such a child will make horrible decisions and will end up looking like something out of a Garanimals commercial—or will always choose chicken nuggets and french fries, becoming malnourished. Indeed, in a way, that's exactly what we're creating—children who are malnourished physically, ethically, emotionally, and psychologically. We see it daily in the way children behave in public and the ways moms react—pleading and placating, rather than taking their child in hand. Parents are giving over to the children the responsibility of raising the children. You hear more amazing tales every day.

Just recently a friend was telling me that she was about to board an airplane with her screaming toddler. What did the mom do? She said, "If you don't stop crying, the pilot's not going to let you get on the airplane." Another mom—this one of a teenager—tells me that she's worried that her daughter is going to parties at homes where there's no parental supervision. This is an entirely legitimate concern in this age of rampant drinking and sexual behavior among teens. But what does the mom do? Does she forbid her child to go to such parties, or at least make a point of calling the partygivers' parents? No—she contacts the school and asks *them* to make a rule that no one can give a party unless there's a parent there.

> It's the parents' job to match the child's level of development to what the child is able to comprehend and do *for himself or herself.*

Then there's what I see every day in my practice. There was a time when no child of 2 or 3 years of age would hit, slap, or pinch a mom: Such behavior was almost unheard of. When I began practicing medicine twenty years ago, I saw a child like that once in a blue moon. Now I see that in 30 percent of my patients—even among the very little ones. They have absolutely no respect for Mom. When I walk in with my lab coat, that might give them a little pause, but if Mom says something they don't like, or if she's not taking them home soon enough, they'll start pinching her where they think I can't see.

How do the moms react? Instead of asserting authority or even saying, "Stop it!" they'll usually say something like "If you don't stop it, the doctor's going to hit you." Or "The doctor is going to give you a very big shot."

This is what they do *right in front of me!*

Naturally, this puts me in a rather awkward position, since the mom has just involved me in her lie. I look at the mom, then at the child, who's now quivering in fear over what I'm about to do. And I've got to tell you—there are times when, having just watched the kid in action, I'm sorely tempted to laugh diabolically and say "Yes! And I'm going to make it the biggest needle I can find!"

Of course, as the child gets older, Mom's having acted as what I call a human vending machine instead of as an authority figure affects others outside the home more and more. Think of it this way: A 3-year-old child with very high self-esteem is merely being a 3-year-old, but when she is still that way at 15 or 18 or 20 years old, she is no longer just Mom's problem: She's a problem for the whole world.

A couple of examples from my own experience:

When my daughter Hannah was in fourth grade, I went to her classroom one evening for Teacher's Night, and sitting at the next desk was the mom of one of Hannah's friends, busily writing sticky notes. "You are an amazing child," read one. "There is no one like you in the entire world." "You are absolutely unique and Mom's little buttercup" went the next. "I can't imagine what my life would be like without you"—and on and on. And then she stuck these notes all around her daughter's desk and in her notebooks so that the girl would be living in an immense bubble of self-esteem.

Self-esteem is a concept we hear often these days, and not just from parents but also from teachers and mental health profession-als—way *too* often. Well-grounded human beings, human beings who have character, develop not on empty praise but rather on reality. Self-esteem, or esteeming oneself, is synonymous with vanity and conceit. These are not characteristics that most mothers desire in their children. What happened to this girl should be no surprise. As she grew older, believing she was a gift from the heavens, she became increasingly rude and demanding—someone other people didn't want to be around. She grew into a personality monster.

I saw another such kid—and her enabling mom—in action over an excruciating several days when I went with my daughter's ninth-grade class to Europe. The mother had relatives in the northern part of the country who had never met her daughter, so these lovely people made the long trip to the city we were visiting, planning to get to know her. But the girl made it clear she wasn't interested in spending her valuable time with them. She didn't want to miss any activities with the other kids, even to be with relatives who had driven an entire day to see her family—and *her mom* totally *let her have her way*. So for two days,

> Mom, do not become a needs vending machine for your child instead of being an authority figure. It is as bad for your child as it is for you.

these lovely people sat around the lobby of the hotel, waiting for this child to make time for them. And even after she finally showed up at

10:00 p.m., she let her family know that she regarded spending her time with them as a chore and a burden.

This was not just appallingly inconsiderate behavior, but it also confirmed her sense that she was the most important person in the world—that other people's feelings simply didn't matter. And in submitting to it, the mother was further distorting both her daughter's character and her daughter's psyche. When such children reach adulthood, they are not prepared to meet the challenges of a difficult life, because they have no coping skills. They have never needed to cope with the world; in their childhood, the world coped with them.

Lately, of course, we're seeing the same thing among some college students—young adults throwing glorified tantrums, making the same demands they made as children and still expecting to get their way. They have never experienced a time when they were not the center of the known universe. Now colleges and universities are packed with emperors in need of subjects. They demand that professors or college presidents step down, and *they actually get their way*—because, like their parents, those who should be in authority have relinquished their power. This is not healthy for our kids, nor for our society.

The results of our changing methods of raising our kids have become all too evident. According to a study of 16,000 college students conducted at San Diego State University in 2006, fully 30 percent were identified in psychological tests as narcissistic, twice as many as were found to be so in a similar study conducted in 1982. Who can doubt that things have gotten even worse since then? Narcissists were defined by the authors of the study as those who, having an "inflated sense of self[,] . . . lacked empathy, were vain and materialistic and had an overblown sense of entitlement."

What's going on here? As a professional matter, I think a lot about what's happening neurologically, in the brains of young people who have been raised in a child-centered parenting style.

What exactly do I mean by that? As parents, we have assumed a style of parenting that forces *us* to take direction from the *child* on when he or she is ready to do certain things, such as sleeping through the night or toilet training. When we take our cues from the child rather than using time-tested developmental milestones, we are actually delaying the development of the child's nervous system and brain. We are also missing the windows of developmental opportunity in the child's development. When these windows are missed, the child will never reach his or her full potential. These days, the pacifier's often still there until the child is 3 years old, toilet training is delayed until 4 years old, and the child doesn't start to self-feed until 3 to 4 years old—and some moms are still cutting the meat up when the child is 8 years old. Compare this to just fifty years ago, when infants were sleeping through the night by the time they were 8 weeks old, the bottle was gone by 1 year old, and toilet training was accomplished by 18 to 24 months of age. This new parenting method sets the child's brain development on a completely different path. This path leads to 5-year-olds' entering kindergarten barely able to control their bodily functions. Is it any wonder that they cannot pay attention to the teacher? This delayed development carries through to high school. Our 18-year-olds have the responsibilities of an adult but the developmental maturity of 12- to 14-year-olds. I believe that this is part of the reason we are seeing such unusual behavior in our schools. Things such as school shootings, cutting, increased depression, and increasingly bizarre suicide methods are the result of this delayed developmental maturity of our kids' brains. We must remember that our children's brains are maturing into their early twenties—and since our child-rearing is not following the correct development path, their brain maturation is lagging.

In other words, this is analogous to what happens when normal physical development is impeded. If, for example, a child isn't sitting up at 6 to 9 months of age, parents will, rightly, be concerned, understanding that those muscles aren't developing properly. Well, it's the same with the brain—it's vital that the neurons of the frontal lobe connect at the right time. If not, the results can be dire. I like to use this example for the parents in my clinic: If an infant is born with congenital cataracts, we understand that we must correct this before the child is about 9 months old. We understand that if it is not corrected by then, the infant, though having an intact eye and optic nerve, will be blind, because the connection between the two has not been made. This is another window of opportunity to connect the brain's pathways. Failing to do so before the window closes has catastrophic consequences.

> Solid human beings who have character are built not on empty praise but on earned respect. No corner cutting!

In this regard, neurologically speaking, those infuriating college students are really 14-year-olds in adult bodies. Somebody has told them *Your petty grievance is not important to the world*, and they're furious—and letting everyone know it.

Chapter Six

. . . OVERPROTECTED . . .

A few years after we started our clinic, a sweet mother and her children joined the practice. Carol was the older girl, and she was very, very smart. In fact, she was the valedictorian of her graduating class of several hundred. But I saw character flaws in this young lady that cast a dark shadow on her future. She was too sure of herself and even a little bit arrogant. These are not traits to foster in an adolescent. She was not honest, and she was not a hard worker. School had come a little too easily for her. This teenage girl was awarded a full scholarship to an excellent four-year private religious college. Her scholarship, including room and board, was worth several hundred thousand dollars. Carol left for school that fall full of hopes and dreams of a life about to begin. She returned a few weeks later because she had already failed out of school. She felt that she was an equal of her professors and tried to tell *them* what to do. She felt that she should not be required to write a theological essay, because "no one should impose their religion on me." The irony of accepting a private scholarship from a private religious college but then objecting to writing a theological essay was lost on her. She had several other run-ins with the authority figures in the college and was sent home. She was an extremely intelligent girl who was not given the tools to be successful in life. She had never been taught to submit to authority, because she was raised in a parenting environment where she was *the* most important person in the room.

High–self-esteem children run into this problem time and time again. Just a few short years later, Carol, the girl of so much promise, has had several children out of wedlock. She is forced to live on government subsidies to survive. Her mom is burdened with Carol's troubles and shares her grief with me when I see her. Each time I see her, she asks me the same question: "What could I have done differently?"

The answer is all too clear. Even as today's kids rule over the house, running roughshod over their moms, they are being shielded from the normal hurts and bruises traditionally associated with childhood, raised as hothouse flowers for whom nothing should ever go wrong. And this, too, impedes their neurological maturity.

Again, we see this clearly in the behavior of today's college students. They act like entitled bullies who think the world should bend to their whims just as their parents did. But they are also fragile snowflakes, unable to withstand any perceived slights. This is why they are constantly demanding "safe spaces" and "hate-free zones," looking for places where they will never be confronted with anything they find shocking, unpleasant, or threatening in any way (including ideas they don't agree with). They're trying to replicate in the real world the homes they grew up in, where they were the center of the universe. In that world, they never had to hear the word *no* or deal with anyone who made them uneasy. Put them outside that comfort zone, and they fall apart.

Of course, these are not actually kids anymore—at least not chronologically. In other generations, they might have already been through wars and be raising families. But, of course, for many people, childhood now extends into the thirties—or even later.

How does it start? A friend from New York tells me that it is common in that trend-setting town to see 3- to 5-year-old children wearing helmets and other protective gear while riding scooters an inch off the ground, creeping along at a snail's pace as anxious parents hover above lest—heaven forbid!—they suffer a tiny scrape. Think of the message being communicated here! What ought to be a simple, fun activity has been converted into one fraught with anxiety! *Mom thinks I might fall! I could hurt myself! There could be pain!*

> Kids learn and grow by living life and sometimes failing. Only by learning to deal with failure do we grow stronger and more capable.

While these moms and dads think they're being wonderful parents, they're really not helping their children develop the skills necessary to get through life. The fact is, you learn by living life—and by sometimes failing. A scraped knee is not a tragedy; it's a valuable lesson.

And, by the way, if a mom feels an activity is so dangerous that she has to put the child in bubble wrap before going outside, perhaps it is better that she not let him do the activity in the first place. Most of the time she does so only because the child himself demands it—and, as we've seen, *no* should not be a dirty word.

So this is a twofer: Even as you're building a child narcissist who expects everyone to bend to his or her will, you're also conveying the sense that everything is a threat—that the entire world should be a safe space.

In short, once again, we are not allowing our kids to mature in a normal and healthy way. Bruises have their purpose: They let you know that brushing them off and keeping going is what it takes to succeed in life.

These days, we hear a lot more than we used to about bullying—and, no question, it certainly *seems* it's worse than ever before, especially since it now also comes in new and different forms, including cyberbullying. And—no question—in the worst cases, it can be awful for those targeted.

But the fact is, bullying has existed as long as there have been people. The difference is that today's kids are just not handling being bullied as well as earlier ones did. We've *disempowered* them by taking away the instruments kids once used to teach themselves to be strong and resilient.

What happens when a kid is confronted with a bully these days? He or she is expected to report it to some authority figure—the teacher or parent—who then has to go and fight the

> Overprotected kids are prevented from maturing in a normal and healthy way. They do not have the tools to become resilient adults.

fight for the kid. Rather than learning how to stand up for himself, he identifies as a victim and hopes someone intervenes on his behalf.

Again, we see the inevitable result on today's campuses. Denied the ability to stand up for themselves, and the tool of self-confidence that comes by doing so, young people feel helpless and break apart.

The fact is, in today's culture, victimhood is reinforced at every turn. Once there was a stigma to it, as there should be. I remember when I was in sixth grade, I started walking around like the world had ended after my best friend moved away—and a couple of Spanish-speaking boys in the neighborhood started teasing me about it. Today we'd call them bullies. They called me *la muerta*, which literally means *the dead girl*, and pretty soon other kids started doing it, calling "Hey, dead girl!" when I passed. When I finally told my mom, she said: "Know what? You're encouraging them with your behavior, because you've earned that name. Instead, when you walk by, put your shoulders up and move confidently, like a young girl with a purpose." Of course, she was right—all it took was to stop *acting* like a victim. But I also did something more. Since I was in the advanced sixth grade class, I looked over my shoulder as I strode by and said, "You know, if you guys were as smart as you are mouthy, maybe you wouldn't be failing sixth grade." That really stopped them in their tracks. Afterward, when I walked by, there was complete silence.

Imagine if my mom had instead walked down the street with me, wagged a finger at those boys on my behalf, and said, "You bad boys, you stop that!" I'm laughing now just thinking about it! But that's just what many moms would do nowadays.

Ronald Reagan used to tell a story about being bullied terribly when he was about 10 years old. It came to a head one day when his mom looked through the kitchen window and saw two bullies chasing him home. She went to the front door and said, "Dutch, we don't run away from our problems. Whatever it takes, you go back and deal with the situation before you come into the house."

That was *his* mom.

So ten minutes later he came back, a little scuffed up, but he'd handled it by settling things himself with those two kids.

Talk about great parenting! What Nelle Reagan was communicating to her son was her absolute confidence that he could handle it. She was communicating strength.

Today? Heck, social services would be there in ten minutes, and she might be arrested. And you know what? Without that lesson, he'd never have grown up to become Ronald Reagan—or, by the way, ever known how to deal with those big Russian bullies.

Of course, parents today seek to protect their children not just from physical hurts and bruises but also from bad grades at school. They're ever vigilant, ready at a moment's notice to intercede on their child's behalf. These kids don't get bad grades, because Mom and Dad won't allow that to happen. How many parents these days "help out" their kids with homework by basically doing it for them? As parents, it is our job to match our children's level of development to what they are able to comprehend and *do for themselves.*

There's one mom I know who is always there, keenly feeling her daughter's every pain, disappointment, and heartache. For her, every B or C her child gets is anguish, and she blames the teacher, because the fault cannot possibly be her daughter's. She actually had a pediatrician put her daughter on a stimulant and then on a second stimulant; then, when neither turned the girl's B's into A's, she arranged for the school to give her daughter extra test time on account of her ADHD "diagnosis."

Anyone can see a disaster down the road for her, but the mom refuses to see it. She honestly believes she's helping her daughter— she insists that she is—but of course she's doing exactly the opposite. Her attitude is *I have to do everything I can to get my daughter into the right college.* But her daughter is not yet complete; the mom hasn't allowed her to experience failure and learn from it. And, of course, the first time the daughter gets an F in college, both daughter and mom will go to pieces.

Little wonder there are schools out there that won't give anything but A's and B's, simply to avoid problems with angry parents. They'll have students repeat a test *until* they earn an A. They simply will not allow a child to experience failure. So they've created a fake world of only success.

> If you've constructed a world where your child cannot fail, that's a fake world.

A mom who does this either has completely lost perspective or has no conception of the basic idea of her job—which is to see to it that her child is given the tools to be able to stand on his or her own two feet as an adult. She is parenting for today, rather than for the long-term, and that is a formula for failure. Children must learn that things do not always go their way and that the world does not revolve around them or their whims. That means you may have to let them go alone to the principal's office or even watch them get fired, recognizing *My kid needs this lesson at this moment.* While your child should know you are there, unless she deals with the reality of that moment and picks herself up, he she won't be able to face far bigger moments down the road.

Only in learning to deal with failure do we grow stronger and more capable. The greatest achievers in the world—explorers, scientists, inventors—all failed at one time or another. They understood that failing at a task didn't mean that they had failed as people, and their temporary setback did not define them. Unfortunately, today's kids are unidimensonal and failure is overwhelming to them.

Indeed, the other part of the message such a mom sends is even more damaging: *I don't think you're capable of succeeding without me at your side.* And she's right—at least right then. At that moment, either the child is not yet developmentally able to successfully complete the task and assignment on his own, or, having been taught to be helpless, the child lacks the confidence to succeed.

But down the road, when a child finds herself on her own in a school or job situation, her reflexive response will be *I can't do this—I need help.* All of a sudden, she is not getting the grade she wants—or the promotion—and doesn't understand why. Why? Because the child is using the same methods that she has always used to get success—and the sudden failure of these methods is traumatic.

A few years ago, I had a nurse practitioner student from a great school come to our clinic for her pediatric rotation. Unfortunately, she was not a hard worker. In fact, she was intent on cutting corners in her education. She would arrive five to fifteen minutes late for work each day. When it was time for her to see a patient, she hid from view. She did, however, make time to look at her phone as much as possible. Her work performance was at the bare minimum. This is not typical of most students that we train. I told her the problems that I was seeing in her work at the clinic and gave her a chance to fix herself. But when the time came for her evaluation, I was forced to give her only satisfactory and a few unsatisfactory grades. She was very upset and walked into the clinic insisting on another face-to-face meeting to discuss her grades. She did this on a busy Saturday morning in the middle of flu season. I told her

> Do not teach your child to feel like a victim—ever. Teach him or her strength, and communicate that strength at all times.

that I was seeing patients but that if she wished to wait, she could do so. She said: "Really? You expect *me* to wait?" I reminded her that she had walked in without an appointment and that it would be unfair to make my patients wait due to her lack of planning. She bristled but decided to wait.

When I finished the busy morning clinic, I called her back to the office. She began: "What do you have against me that you want me to fail?" When I asked her to explain further, she went on: "My work here has not been any worse than on my other rotations. Why are you picking on me?" Of course, I was not picking on her. It seemed that I was the only one of her professors who was willing to grade her on the work that she actually did. Rather than perform a self-evaluation of her poor work effort, she shifted the blame onto another (me).

Not long ago, I was sitting in a plane beside a very nice woman who does medical school admissions at a university in my area, as well as counseling of students already admitted, and she was telling me of a new phenomenon she has been seeing in the past several years. Students in the second year of medical school, adults aged 23 to 26 years, have been coming to her office, saying, "I don't know if I can do this. You have to help me."

The first year, there was one such student; a year later, three; the year after that, seven. Today, she said, she sees it approaching 50 percent of the medical school class. Now some parents have gotten involved in their adult children's medical school career. They call her, demanding, "What are you going to do to help my child?"

So she said that what they've done in response to this problem—which has never before occurred in medical school—is create a no-fail system. These students are able to continue taking exams until they pass.

Really? Is *that* what we want in our doctors? Will we next want airline pilots who have never been allowed to fail?

The truth is that kids are immensely capable if only we raise them properly and give them the opportunity to grow. More important, kids are not just capable but also resilient. During World War II, in occupied Europe, it was the kids who adjusted best to those terrible circumstances. Adults often came out so broken that they could no longer function, but kids in the same situation were usually able to overcome their circumstances and go on.

It has always been this way. A friend tells me about her great-grandfather, who, during the Civil War, was sent alone, as an 11-year-old, from Connecticut to Washington, D.C., to tend for his wounded father. The mother expected that he would make the journey and return with his father. He did.

Obviously, I'm not advocating sending 11-year-olds off by themselves to care for injured parents, but there's no question that we're thwarting today's kids by not giving them real responsibilities. We either don't expect enough of them or

> A parent's job is to launch a child into the world able to stand on his or her own two feet: *That's* parenting for the long term.

expect the wrong things. What we've done is taken capable children and removed the real, concrete problems they should experience. These experiences are necessary for them to overcome obstacles and learn the lessons of success. Instead, we have replaced these experiences with small, inconsequential tasks that we won't even let them solve on their own. Then we give them a participation trophy and write *Champion* on it. This is not healthy for the development of our children.

I look at my daughter Hannah, now 16 years old, and there's one thing that makes me especially proud as a mom. She's not the best student in the world, nor the best athlete. But what I hear from people all the time—and I take it as a great compliment—is that she's *sturdy*. That's the word they use: *sturdy*. That's what you strive for when you build a kid: the capacity to get up and dust yourself off when things don't go your way. So when Hannah has a momentary setback—say, fails to grab a key rebound in an important game—it's no big deal, because we know how quickly she'll bounce back (in a much more important sense) from *that*.

Chapter Seven

. . . AND (DEFINITELY) OVERSTRESSED . . .

*J*t's almost too easy to make fun of all those students on today's college campuses who are constantly throwing tantrums—from afar, those places seem less like institutions of higher learning than mammoth playpens. You think *Wow, what happened? You can't cope with* what? *Going to college and having fun?*

But it's important also to remember that to those young people, their "issues" and "demands"—from the anxiety produced by ideas they don't agree with to the pleas for "safe spaces"—are legitimate and strongly felt. As a result of a lifetime of exposure to incorrect parenting, they truly have been *made* fragile, stressed in ways that prior generations could never have imagined.

When a boy I know was a senior in high school, a strapping six-foot-two, handsome, and talented—not to mention a good student—he'd already been accepted at a very good school. Suddenly, he started doing poorly in all his subjects. Instead of going off to college, he had to enter rehab and ultimately was admitted to a psychiatric ward.

The obvious question: *What happened?*

He realized: *I am 18, and I have to leave home—and I am not ready.* He felt emotionally incapable. Having been cosseted by his mom, protected from life's challenges, he found the very thought terrifying. He wanted to remain in a situation in which he had to be cared for.

> Don't put your child in the position of making decisions that he or she isn't neurologically able to make.

This was an extreme case, but it makes a point that applies to a lot of kids and their parents these days: If the job isn't done right by the time the child is supposed to launch, he will stall—and sometimes crash and burn. You can be 18 years old but emotionally still be 12 or 13 years old.

The problem is that he wasn't brought up to maturity, and if you turn such a child out into the world, that child isn't going to make it. He may just need an extra year of maturing—not sitting on the couch but rather being responsible, having a job and learning to manage money. Perhaps he could take a couple of community college courses. But however it's done and whatever it takes, what's key is raising that child to maturity.

Sometimes the results of stress are even more tragic. I remember reading a few years ago about a sudden rash of teen suicides in Palo Alto, California, home of Stanford University and one of the most affluent communities anywhere. Eleventh- and twelfth-graders, a number of them on the honor roll, were throwing themselves in front of trains. Their parents were university professors and highly paid professionals. And that was just an especially dramatic version of a widespread reality: Suicide is now the second most prevalent cause of death among American teens. Indeed, according to the Centers for Disease Control and Prevention, one in six high school students has seriously considered suicide, and one in twelve has actually attempted it.

Quite simply, these kids are undergoing stresses that other generations of kids never had; they are children who from the earliest age were put in the position of *making a whole bunch of decisions for themselves that they were not neurologically ready to make.* And then, too often, they were given far too much power in their own homes. Their parents have used a parenting method that allows children to make decisions they are not yet capable of making. Such children have been allowed to experience life rather than being guided by their parents. Then, to preserve their self-esteem, their parents never allowed them to fail. This gave them too little opportunity to make basic mistakes and to endure the resilience-breeding failures they needed for proper maturation.

Besides that, many children find themselves under the ultimate pressure: They feel responsible for their *parents'* happiness. So many moms I see now are living their lives vicariously, through their children. Only through their kid's successes do they feel validated. They communicate the message *You complete me,* which is a very dangerous position to put a child in. It creates enormous anguish, and it places an immense and unfair responsibility on the child.

This syndrome always existed, to a certain extent, but it was never nearly so prevalent as it is today. In earlier generations, parents loved their kids, but they didn't draw their strength and sense of well-being from their children's success.

These days, even when a child "succeeds," the question often becomes *Whose success is it?*

Nor can the child even rebel—at least not in healthy ways—for doing so would be too painful for the parent! So time after time, even kids who from afar look like they're succeeding are in fact living in a very fragile world. Let one little thing go wrong—a failure in school or on the athletic field—and they fall apart.

Parents who use this new parenting method are also putting the child in a position in which the home's happiness and stability depend on her. The child chooses what to eat and where to eat, as well as when to go on vacation and where. In the past, the parents decided these things so that choices would be made in the best interest of the child and the family. Now the burden of happiness rests on the small shoulders of a child. This is pressure that the child never should be burdened with.

One result has been a massive increase in self-destructive behaviors, such as anorexia. Those are kids trying to meet a standard of absolute perfection, which of course is impossible to do. It's no accident that those kids also tend to be very good students, and they're often musical or avid athletes—from the outside, all-around "good kids." They're not troublemakers; they don't misbehave. They have a good amount of drive. I don't think I've met an anorexic kid who wasn't interested in getting ahead. They're usually self-reliant. But that's just the surface. A child who has anorexia has an overwhelming need to be in control of her world so it

> Be careful not to live your life vicariously through your child. You are not validated by your child's success.

won't fall apart, but the only balance she finds is in controlling her own body. Such a child tells herself *If I just stop eating, at least I can meet one level of perfection.*

It comes from trying to fulfill Mom's expectations for the perfect kid.

There's also been a serious increase in self-mutilation, now often referred to as "cutting." Until recently we never saw it in kids, and anyone who self-mutilated would be considered psychopathic. To be clear, the children of the past were rarely, if ever, psychopathic. Now I see a child like that every two or three months, and they come from every income and population group. Why would a 12- or 14-year-old be cutting himself or herself? Again, it comes down to a kid who labors under very high expectations and who doesn't know how to manage frustrations, having never been given the proper coping mechanism. It's an outward expression of what the child is feeling inside—anger and resentment and self-pity—at not having the emotional or psychological tools to deal with the world.

> It is not your child's job to make sure you're happy.

And that's how I, as a professional, have to deal with these kids—because only by acknowledging that anger and resentment can you break through. Only then can I begin to teach the child and the parent methods for coping with these feelings.

Some time ago I had an emergency situation. The mom had rushed over after getting a call from her 12-year-old's middle school—the girl was scratching herself and making herself bleed. We dropped everything, pushing aside other appointments, because this situation was so dire. The mom was in tears, the girl very angry and resentful.

Why was she cutting herself? It turned out that her birth father had left the home, and her mother had remarried. Now there was a new kid in the home whom she felt had taken over the limelight.

This girl had always been very controlling, a real CEO in the making, pushing back against her mom, but now she felt as if no one was listening to her. She'd always been a good student, but beyond her acting out at home—screaming, yelling, and slamming doors—her grades had begun to suffer. This affected the whole family. If she was behaving, everything was fine; if not, everything was chaos. The family's sense of well-being—and the girl's mom's—was totally her responsibility and under her control.

I had to interrupt this vicious cycle. We had to restore the correct balance in the mom's relationship with her daughter. After we had talked for a while, we stopped to pray: We wanted to give those bad feelings to God to help this girl cope with them. Afterward, I told her she wasn't a second-class citizen in the home and never had been. Her mom had an incredibly special, unique love for her that would never go away. Hearing this, the child started crying. She felt a burden lifted from her, understanding that it was not her place in life to make her mom happy. And the cutting stopped immediately. She and her mom just needed that kind of refocusing. She had to stop creating chaos, and Mom had to stop responding to the moment-to-moment drama and focus on the long view instead. When the girl's power to disrupt was taken away, she was reestablished as just another kid in the home.

> Children need to learn *proper* coping mechanisms for dealing with frustration.

It's so gratifying to have that kind of result—to really reach a child and to see her change and start to grow up and thrive as she should.

The key, as always, was making her place in the family clear and secure by putting the roles of parents and child in the right balance.

Chapter Eight

THE TIE THAT BINDS—
OR THAT SHOULD

*O*ne thought that I often mull over during our drive to the practice is: *What happened to that glue that used to cement our society? How did we allow things to stray so far away from the successful way we used to raise our children?* I have yet to meet an 80- or 90-year-old mom who tells me of the great anxiety and difficulty she had raising her children. It just did not happen. Early in my medical career, I wondered if these women were made of sturdier stuff than the women of today.

I grieve to think of one of our little boys, Karl. His mom seems incapable of seeing how important she is to the success of her son. He is a smart kid and a great athlete. Mom only sees the Karl who is misbehaving at school and who is "unable to focus." "He just needs some medicine," she tells me. I hear this frequently from this type of mom. When I explained that he doesn't need medicine but *does* need her to parent differently, she became openly hostile. She does *not* feel that she plays a role in his development or success as a child. He truly is "not my problem," she says. When she made this statement, I looked at Karl. He gave me a look that broke my heart. All I can do is help to instruct her and pray that she gets it. "It" is supposed to be "a mom thing," but it wasn't on that day in my examination room.

Getting the family roles in order almost always begins with fixing something terribly important and recently forgotten: restoring the mother–child bond. Indeed, by far the biggest reason so many moms today feel such anxiety and distress is that they've allowed that bond to unravel.

> A successful mother–child bond keeps you in sync with your child, letting you know his or her strengths and weaknesses, where he or she needs to be challenged, and how you can help him or her.

What is it, exactly? That so many moms have to ask is maybe the surest sign of the depth of the problem. Not so many years ago, the sure sense of intuition that is its essence arrived with the birth of a child and never left. Now, in too many cases, it never forms or has vanished.

Once moms parented with confidence, certain of their instincts and guided by a strong inner voice. They knew that they were in charge and knew how to make decisions for their children that were age- and developmentally appropriate, and so they also knew when it was time to start cutting the cord, giving children room to grow and properly mature.

Moreover, moms knew with absolute certainty that they could not live vicariously through their children and should never try to do so. If they did, the kids would almost certainly suffer.

Today, far too many of us have lost the ability to hear that inner voice—or, if we do, to decipher it clearly.

I deal with such moms every day in my practice. My aim is to help them retrieve the mother–child bond and thus their relationship with their kids. It's never too late to restitch that bond, but there's no question that doing so gets harder with time.

The first thing that moms—and dads, too—have to understand is how drastically the family itself has changed in recent years and how that is affecting our kids. As recently as a couple of generations ago, the respective parental roles were clear and unquestioned. It was understood not just that child-rearing was primarily the mom's responsibility but also that the relationship had unquestioned rules and parameters: The mom had the power, and the children paid her unwavering respect. This was the basis of the very strong, tangible parent–child bond in most families—one that, indeed, transcended the family unit; it was nothing less than the glue holding society itself together.

Not that the mother–child bond was created by society. To the contrary, it is a gift from God. It begins at birth—in fact, even before birth. While there's no question that an adopted child who has loving parents will thrive, the strongest bond a newborn will have is with his or her mother. That's why it's better to breastfeed. Make sure to look at your baby's eyes when he or she is born and when you're nursing. It's an emotional, elemental thing. It kindles the relationship. That bond exists to help you love your child, makes it so that you are literally ready to die for this little human being who is so innocent and so helpless. It is an amazing thing to see and gives me joy in my job as a pediatrician.

At the same time, it's essential to develop a longer-term perspective. You start with a bond that is very real, yet very much for the moment. In this way, the mother–child bond has something in common with the love between a man and a woman: At the start, it flames and smolders, but gradually it evolves, becoming something different. A successful mother–child bond is one in which you remain in sync with your child, knowing him or her so intimately you are always aware of what your child's strengths and weaknesses are, where and how you can help him or her, but also where he or she needs to be challenged—and, as a result, one in which your child continues to regard *you* with real and unalterable respect.

Why has that bond frayed so badly?

A huge factor in that fraying is the babble of voices in today's culture telling moms different—and often contradictory—things. One of the loudest is the hectoring voice of the government: *You don't know how to feed your child properly and nutritionally; let the school do it. When your child experiences loss or trauma—has lost a grandmother or suffered the tragic death of a school* friend—*you don't know how to comfort your child; bring in counselors or psychologists. Your child isn't yet speaking or reading as well as others; turn to a speech or reading specialist.*

And that's before we even get to Common Core and how it greatly increases stress on many children by putting in place standards that fail to match the stages of a child's development. Yet most moms quietly defer to the "authorities" of child-rearing, medicine, and psychiatry, lacking the self-confidence to challenge the "experts." They do this against their maternal instinct, because deep down, they know that there is something wrong with how their children are being taught.

This incessant *drip, drip, drip* starts eroding the mother–child bond from the very beginning. It doesn't take long for the average mom to start second-guessing herself. Her child might say *wabbit* instead of *rabbit*, and instead of brushing it off, she begins to worry: *I don't know how fix it—I'd better take her to a speech therapist.* To be sure, in certain situations, there's nothing wrong with a speech therapist. The problem is that in today's America, the message internalized by moms is *You can't do this by yourself. Without somebody else, you're lost. Your child will be lost. Without a special school counselor, your child won't be able to find a career or get through life.*

Amid this constant onslaught, the challenge for the child's mother is finding a way to sit quietly and sort through all the noise. Sure, she can ask for advice; no one knows everything about everything. Still, the way to maintain the crucial mother–child bond is to be absolutely certain of one thing: *I know my kid best.* I would like moms to square their shoulders and understand that there's simply nobody better for your child than you are. No flotilla of experts is going to raise that kid better than you—if only you'd take the reins.

> You know your child better than anyone else.

In that sense, we're all experts. A parent can and should draw on his or her own childhood experiences. We remember how, as kids, we had the same sorts of problems. So you don't need a therapist; you need to tell your child: "This is what you do in that situation—and you respect yourself."

I'm only grateful this obsession with so-called experts wasn't the norm when I was little. Back then, I slurred my Ss a bit, and I had a slight lisp. That's not a speech delay—it's a weakness of the tongue.

Of course, there will be exceptions in which the mom is absolutely, positively not in a position to raise her child: a mother on drugs, for example, or a mother who is psychiatrically incapable of taking care of her child. Those cases exist, and society must help. We will mentor, foster, and carry that child—whatever it takes.

But I'm not talking to that mom at this moment. I'm talking to the mom who has come to feel *I'm incapable.* I want to reassure her: *No, you* are *capable.* But the first thing we have to do is restore that mother–child bond. Learn to shut out the voice that says *I can't do this,* and feel the power from within. I want her to understand that *nobody* can help her child the way she can.

In the office, moms often tear up when I tell them this—and Jane's mom was no exception. Jane's mom was in the office while I was writing this book. Jane was uncontrollable in the exam room while waiting for her sick visit appointment. Jane is 3 years old and throws terrible temper tantrums to get her way. She is very intelligent and plays her mom like a concert violinist plays her instrument. This day was no different. Jane did not want to be in my exam room. When I walked into the room after hearing the commotion from outside the door, I took command, and Jane calmed down immediately. Jane's mom exclaimed, "Can we take you home with us?"

I explained to Jane's mom that she, not I, was the perfect mother for Jane. It was her maternal voice, not mine, that was best suited for Jane's life and successful future. I explained to her that she could do what I just did, but far better. First, she must believe it. Then, she must act like it. If she could not feel it, then she should copy me and fake it. Soon, the mother who was acting as the understudy would become the leading lady. When Mom acts on this reality, it will change Jane's future forever.

> There's no one better for your child than you.

Chapter Nine

MEET THE LITTLE TYRANT

How badly is the mother–child bond frayed? I see the answer every day at the clinic.

One of my rules of thumb is that today's tantrum has its roots in yesterday's parenting. If your child is throwing tantrums at age 7, then he is developmentally aged 2 or 3. Your child's behavior needs to be rolled back. He needs to be reeducated so that he is a 7-year-old not just in body but also in mind.

Instead, as I see every day, parents make excuses for their kids—and, by extension, for themselves. I don't know how many times I've heard a mom say: "Everyone says my kid's just going through a phase." Or: "I couldn't do that—it would feel like I was being *mean*."

It's time to roll all that back. The emotional tsunami in your home did not come from nowhere. Make no mistake: When a child is acting out, it is because of how he or she has been trained by Mom and Dad to behave. The parents have surrendered their power to their children.

What follows is one particularly severe case—which, for that very reason, is especially revealing. This little guy is 3 years old, and we can also

> Today's tantrum has its roots in yesterday's parenting.

call him the Little Tyrant, because that really gets to the heart of it.

This is how I met him. One day, I'm sitting at my desk doing administrative stuff, and one of my doctors comes back, saying she needs help with a patient. A mother had shown up without an appointment, and she was distraught. Her complaint was all too familiar: "I just don't know what to do about this boy anymore."

Both Dan and his mother looked like they've been crying, but the mom looks even more upset than the little boy. It turns out they've come directly from his daycare, which has kicked him out. And this isn't the first time: It has happened twice before at other places.

The mother is so upset, very nervous and continually breaking down, that she can hardly get the story out. "Listen," I tell her, "I know it looks really bad right now, but I'm sure we can get to the bottom of it. If you tell me the story, we can figure out where it started and how I can help you."

So she tells me that she'd just started him in a little private in-home daycare—just three or four other kids, all about his age. And right from the start, he'd been baiting the daycare worker, making fun of her behind her back to the other kids.

And it had continually been escalating—because that is what these kids do, even at a very young age: They see how much they can get away with. That's how these little manipulators work. They figure out how many buttons they can push, and which, as well as how much they can manipulate.

Dan was obviously a very bright kid and a natural leader, because his button pushing was especially ingenious. So this is what he'd pulled today: He'd arranged that after the daycare lady walked out of the room, every time she came back in, the kids would all cover their mouths, point at her, and laugh.

The mom was still crying as she's telling this, but she described the scene so vividly—these 3- and 4-year-olds all covering their mouths, giggling wildly and pointing—that it was hard not to laugh myself.

And of course Dan is the ringleader. Talk about potential! Imagine understanding at 3 years old that covering your mouth, pointing at someone, and laughing would be demeaning and hurtful. This kid is brilliant!

Meanwhile, the daycare worker, who clearly took herself too seriously, responded exactly the way a kid like that would hope. She got angry and started shouting, "You guys stop that!" Of course, that only made them giggle more.

A little later, she served them grapes, and when she left the room for a moment, Dan pulled his next trick. Who knows exactly what he said, but it was along the lines of *Okay, when she comes back, we're going to all throw the grapes at her.* Because that's exactly what happened. As soon as she walked in, he shouted, "Throw!" and they did. At that, the worker lost it and started screaming at them—at which point Dan calls for another volley.

The woman shouts, "That's it! You're done!" And she jerks Dan up by the arm, grabs the phone, and calls his mom, telling her, "You'd better leave your job right now and pick this kid up, because we're through."

Half an hour later, with no appointment, Dan's mom screeches into our parking lot. Aside from everything else, she's terrified she's going to lose her job, because her boss has warned her that she can't just be taking off like this—and that she'd better be back soon. A single mom, she needs her paycheck, and she can see the dominoes falling: Her livelihood, her sanity, and her future are all on the line here. But even more so, her little boy's future is on the line. Nobody wants him, and he's only 3 years old.

So what are we going to do for Dan's mom—and for Dan?

This was a long-term proposition. While today she had to figure out how to take care of the daycare situation and get back to work, she was looking for a lot more than just *Fix my child right now.*

So that's where we were. The mom was looking at me, beseeching. She had a notepad and pencil, ready to take notes. She keeps telling him what to do, but he doesn't do it. Her threats are meaningless, and so is her anger—he keeps acting the same way. What is the solution? I'm the parenting expert—the guru. What do I have to do?

> Do not surrender your power to your child. As parents, we must *never* negotiate with tiny terrorists.

The problem was obvious: The mother–child bond was completely gone, and Dan had filled the power vacuum in the home—so now he was trying to do the same in the world. Already today, he'd not only caused turmoil at his daycare and gotten his mother in trouble with her boss, but he'd also totally disrupted our day at the clinic. This little 3-year-old had caused this incredible, ridiculous sequence of events all because no one has imposed control or order on his life.

It was a worst-case version of the most common problem I face. It's what things look like when parents abdicate control to children.

The mom in such a situation is almost always very anxious and stressed. This is true across the board, from single moms to married moms who have supportive husbands; in fact, sometimes having a partner makes things even harder, since the husband or boyfriend is getting on Mom's case for not doing it right. The common denominator is knowing things have spun out of control but not knowing why. Often Mom has read all the literature out there, assimilated it, and tried to practice it—but without benefit. The more Mom tries to do, the less her child behaves.

So moms are fighting themselves, beating themselves up: *He's just a 5-year-old. Why can't I raise a five-year-old? It's not like it's rocket science. But if I don't do something about it, not only am I going to lose my sanity, but this kid is going to wind up a disaster.*

That's usually where the mom is when I meet her. She's pulling her hair out, losing her sanity. She feels like she's circling the drain.

So where do you begin? Start by understanding that yes, it has been a failure, but it's not a *moral* failure; it's a failure of *tactics*. You've got a kid who is taking over the parental role, with the parent as appeaser. The child is the center of the home, and the mom is merely in reactive mode. That has to change.

As parents, we must *never* negotiate with tiny terrorists! When you engage the tiny terrorist driving your child's disruptive behavior, trying to negotiate with it, you're giving the terrorist the attention and respect that will make it stronger. In this negotiation, your home

> A child **needs** the parent to be in charge. Establish who's the boss—*you*—and stick with it.

is the hostage—and so, in a very real way, is your child's future. It's okay if early on, the consequences sometimes seem disproportionate to the crime. What's vital is taking the reins and shutting things down—period. Dire consequences--figuratively administering an electric shock that resets your child's brain.

In this case, the answer to the question *Who's in charge?* couldn't be simpler: Dan was in charge—and not the developing Dan, the Dan on his way to being a rational, functioning and contributing member of the community, but a *Lord of the Flies* Dan.

When I see a kid like this, exhibiting such unbridled, unchanneled energy, I see amazing raw talent! But I don't recall *Lord of the Flies* for nothing. Already, at 3 years old, the question was whether he would use it for good or for evil—because it could go either way. And he wasn't off to a good start. It's a small jump from there to being a little smart-aleck of 12 or 14 years old who thinks nothing of mouthing off to a police officer, or worse, then ends up getting tried as an adult, throwing away any possibility of a successful, productive life in a mere snap of the fingers. It was up to us to help Dan channel his energy for good rather than letting him use that power to self-destruct.

Where do you start? Start by understanding that a child *needs* his parent to be in charge. I believe that the kid is not bad. His energy and potential just haven't been properly channeled. Most important, the pathways of a child's developing brain are forming in an unhealthy way. He is like a rampaging, out-of-control river, sweeping before it everything in its path—a potential force for good turned dangerous and unpredictable.

And so, with Dan's mom, I began by saying, "You have to start acting like the boss—and *looking* like the boss. Right now you don't, and Dan is taking full advantage of that fact."

She said, "That's *it?*"

"That's it. Because if you don't act like the boss, why would Dan trust you to *be* the boss? He doesn't—and he's right not to. Right now, you're more like his employee. You've sent him the message that he is in charge—that Mom is not strong.

"What's worse is that he's gotten the message that the women in his world are weak and that if he pushes the right buttons, he will always be in charge. So already, at 3 years old, every woman he comes in contact with is perceived as weak and small and easily manipulated.

"And this," I concluded, "is what has you in this room right now."

So, then, the inevitable question: "How do I fix it?"

"As his mom," I told her, "you're going to have to find the particulars of your solution. But first, you have to *feel* you can do it. You have to act like it, and you have to look like it. And if you don't believe it, you're going to have to sit in front of the mirror and model doing it."

> Put on your "boss face," and speak with your "boss voice."

Basically, what I was conveying was that she was going to have to undo everything she'd been doing wrong until now—all that bad behavioral conditioning. And it wasn't going to be simple; there was no magic formula or quick fix. But she had to begin establishing who was the boss and stick with it.

"So look in the mirror and find the boss in you," I said. "You must develop your boss face. Do you *look* like you're in charge? Would *you* listen to you? Look at your physical body language, because that's what kids pick up on first. Are you standing like an authority figure? Listen to the tones that you use to speak to your child. Are your sentences questioning and giving the child a choice, or are they directive and instructing? Do you sound like there's any wiggle room for the child?"

It's hard to overstate how vital it is, this idea of presenting yourself as the authority figure. I remember how it was in my house when I was a kid—how I always knew how I stood with my dad, how I would hear it in his voice. I'd be like: "I'm not even going to ask, because I could hear from the tone of his voice that there'd be hell to pay if I crossed him!" Nobody hit me—nobody punished me— because nobody *had* to. Hell to pay was disappointing someone, and that was the worst punishment of all. When you've messaged your child properly, you don't always need to do much more than that.

So, ideally, that's what you aim for with every child. But, of course, with Dan, we were so far from that point that his mom couldn't even imagine getting there.

Interestingly, black moms, and usually single moms, often have less trouble grasping the idea of the boss face. It's because they've learned to put it on in other areas of their lives. For instance, they know that when they stand in line at Walmart or go to the bank, they're more likely than other people to be short-changed by someone saying they paid with a five instead of a twenty. So they go with a face already in place that says *Don't even think of messing with me.* And it's easy to convey to them that they need to use that same *Don't mess with me* face with their kids.

The attitude has to be *You are his mother, and you mean business. He does not need you to be his friend. You do not need him to like you. You need him to do what you say—period.*

Simple as this sounds, Dan's mom had an especially tough time grasping it. "But what do I *do?*" she asked again.

> Don't make threats; enforce consequences.

"You didn't get what I mean. You start by appearing to be in charge. The demeanor of your being in charge is the

78

first thing that's going to shock him back into starting to act the right way."

"But he's not going to. He will try me. What am I going to do then?"

"Look: So far, everything I've heard from you has been about making excuses—for him and for yourself. You're always threatening. Threat, threat, threat, threat, threat—this spiral of endless, empty threat—and finally you blow up."

"So you're telling me I have to spank him and throw things?"

"No, I'm telling you that you don't threaten, you *do*. Not threats, but consequences."

But she's still shaking her head, as if to say *That's it? That's all she's going to tell me?*

"But I tell him, and he doesn't listen," she starts again.

"Why should he? It doesn't mean anything. Your words are not backed up with action. They are just noise to your child. It is the *action* that he remembers the next day. If you had used this proven parenting technique from early childhood, your child and family wouldn't be at this point now. But that's water under the bridge, because you're going to start doing it now."

So we keep going over this for the better part of an hour, and finally she seems to grasp it and begins feeling a little better. She's not crying anymore, her face isn't quite as red, and there's a glimmer of hope at the end of the tunnel. We've figured out a temporary fix for the work problem—tomorrow she's going to leave Dan with a distant aunt—and she's saying *Okay—I can do this.*

And she's also started to get some perspective. Because her kid is tough and incredibly strong-willed, she has to keep an *I can do this* mentality front and center lest he roll right over her. But, by the same token, those very traits give him a world of potential. Obviously, he's a born leader. Mold him right, have him join us on the side of light, and she will have an amazing human being on her hands—a civic leader or CEO, someone who uses his powers for good.

Otherwise, the Little Tyrant would grow up to be Lex Luthor.

I told her, using the most charitable terms, that right now Dan thought of himself as the Little General. He had been allowed to assume that role far too early, and he played it wherever he went. "Your job is to see to it he's demoted. He needs, at this point, to be the Little Private who learns to take orders, and then he can gradually ascend through the ranks as he grows toward manhood. He's the smartest little guy, but it's up to you to bring that out in him. He can be a general when he's a parent himself."

The alternative? We've all heard too many of those stories of unbridled potential gone wrong. Too many stories of children who heard *yes* when the answer should have been *no*. The result? If he wants that bicycle, he takes it. If he wants a perfect score on that test, he cheats. He takes only yes for an answer.

I've seen it so often first-hand. I have one 15-year-old I've been seeing since he was born—let's call him Brett. When this little guy was born, I had just moved to North Carolina, and I was called to the hospital to take a look at him. The whole extended family was there, all these big gals and all the men in their duck outfits and boots, and they were just the nicest people, all delighted by this baby. But along the way, something went badly wrong. Unfortunately, the guy the mom had chosen for a husband had emotional issues. Before a year or two had passed, he was in and out of the home, throwing things, violent, and abusive. When they finally threw the guy out of the house, the whole family banded together, and they took her in and raised this little guy together.

But of course all this had a terrible effect on Brett. His mom was afraid to be an authority figure and would never say no, so now the boy continuously pushes her around, saying all kinds of mean things to her and throwing things at her when she doesn't do exactly what he wanted. No question—the way things are going, he's going to wind up treating his mom in a completely unacceptable way—or his teacher, or, someday, his

> Don't make threats; keep your *I can do this* mentality front and center.

wife. He was allowed to think that this way of treating women was acceptable because Mom never corrected his behavior.

When I see him now—because his mom still brings him to see me for checkups—I think *Where has my little Brett gone?* And I tell him, "Brett, we've got to change this track you're on, because you're on the same track as your dad—but you don't have to be. But you're the only one who has the ability to stop this." That's what it's come down to for this boy who was once so sweet, who had such unbridled power and possibility.

In raising a child, you're forming not only a heart but also a brain. If you encourage pathways that lead toward aggression, manipulation, lying, and dishonesty, then over the years, it becomes increasingly hard to reroute your child from them. The thread becomes so knotted and tangled that it can no longer be unraveled. Antisocial behavior becomes hardwired.

I hope that it's not too late for Brett, at 15 years old, to be pointed in a different direction—but I honestly don't know. With Dan, however, there's no doubt: The chances of nipping it in the bud are 100 percent.

"I know you have your doubts," I assured his mom, "and I know it's hard to believe today, but it will have a happy ending. Because I have no doubt you can do this. Someday you're going to tell the story of the havoc he caused in daycare, and it will have been the changing moment in Dan's life."

SCRAPBOOK

Rose Baby Picture

Dave and I on our wedding day.

Dave and I when we were dating at Ft. Campbell KY. He looked so hansome in his Dress Blues!

This is a picture of Hannah and me taken a few days after she was born. We lost her first newborn pictures. Dave opened up the camera with the film still in it. He still gets the blame for this to this day!

Hannah at 4 months playing the keyboard with Mom. She plays the guitar now.

Rose and
Hannah (3)

With Mom and
Hannah on the Blue
Ridge. We love the
outdoors and hiking.

With Hannah and my French Canadian "Mom and Dad",
Marielle and Jacques Bureau.
We still see each other several times a year.

With Richard Petty, The King of Racing!

In 2008 Dave and, along with my good friend
Brenda Barr, Dave and I started our own after
school tutoring program, called the Mustard
Seed. Here are some of my girls.

At the practice with the Navarrete Family. Sherman, the youngest, is one of the most beloved patients. He makes us all smile whenever he visits us!

On a local radio show, talking about parenting.

Talking to Middle schoolers about success.

With Dr. Ben Carson.
Dave and I help him with medical policy.

Hannah and I love traveling together and learning about different cultures. We visited Rome last year on a school trip.

We spent this last Christmas in the North Carolina mountains. It is one of our favorite places in the world.

Chapter Ten

RESTORING THE MOTHER–CHILD BOND

Working with Dan involved, more than anything else, working on his mom, which is usually the way it goes. So invested are some moms in the idea that they are in the right and that the problem is their kid that it takes a great deal of time to get them to buy into new ideas in order to help them save their child. For instance, there's the case of 9-year-old Josh, whom I've come to think of as my little basketball guy, and his mother. This mom is herself a product of a single-mother home, and she is raising Josh alone, without a consistent male role model. He sees his grandfather sometimes, but Granddad is an invalid, unable to do much. This boy is in a home that by anybody's standards is not offering him everything that is optimal for his development. There are so many things stacked against him.

But at the same time, Josh has got a lot going for him. He's a good-looking boy and has a beautiful smile. He's very polite and well-behaved at the clinic. He's also terrific at basketball.

Though Josh gives his mom a lot of trouble, I wanted his mom not to obsess on the negative. I wanted her to recognize his assets and develop eyes to see his abilities and the future that he has.

But, as is so often the case, it was really difficult getting her to adopt a mindset from which she could start to reweave that broken fabric. Josh's mom is just exhausted. She works two jobs, and she doesn't feel that she's got it in her to continue the battle. And yes—I feel for her. But if we're asking Josh to give it all he's got, it's crucial that she also dig deeper and do the same.

Since it had been about four weeks since school had started, I started by asking how Josh was doing at school. His mom looked at me with pursed her lips and said, "I haven't heard from the teacher—yet. But I'm expecting to, since nothing's really changed in his behavior."

"Well," I said, "the first thing I want you to think about is your attitude toward your boy. You gave birth to a boy who's going to be a man, and the world will never be completely the same because you brought him into the world. I want you to be positive about that, because you can be such a great influence on this boy. And this boy can be such a wonderful influence in this world. You don't know what he's supposed to be, so I need you to work on your attitude and your abilities to be a mom."

> Don't obsess on negatives. Recognize your child's assets.

As we talked, I could see she was getting frustrated. She wanted to talk about increasing the dosage of the stimulant he's on. She noticed that he acted up in the afternoon, and she was having a lot of trouble getting him through his homework. They'd sit there for an hour working, and then he'd hit a wall and announce, "I can't do this!" Things spiraled out of control, going downhill from there. So Mom wanted a different dose of stimulant—enough to last until they were done with the homework. Instead of doing that, I wanted to better develop her skills as a mom so that she could help him focus better.

"Why do you keep thinking that it's *me* that has to be fixed?" she insisted. "Why can't you just fix *him*, so that he can be a better kid?" Mind you, Josh was sitting there, listening to this, and my heart just broke for him. He gave me a look that said: *See what I have to deal with?*

There was no way for me to make her understand how badly that mother–child bond had frayed, nor that we were dealing with the consequences of its having frayed. If that bond were stronger, she would see why her boy was struggling and would become better able to understand the ways he needs help.

What she needed was to regain access to that inner voice.

"Look," I finally told her, "if you're just looking for another dose of Ritalin or some other stimulant, I'm really not sure I can give you what you want. There are plenty of doctors out there who will do that. There are medications that will help him to filter out the things that are going on around him and pay more attention. But even if you get just the right medicine, it will only be a temporary fix. It won't fix the underlying problem, just the symptom. It'll last a month or six weeks, but then you'll be back here, because he'll have outgrown the medication, and he'll need something else. Then you'll be asking for that something else.

"What we need to do is get to the root of the problem. If I can't stimulate that voice in you, then I'm afraid we're probably not going to be able to truly help your son."

It was a difficult, blunt speech, and when I finished I was thinking *I won't be surprised if she walks out the door and never comes back.* But then I looked over at Josh, and I thought *But if she does, who will give that little guy a helping hand? And who will help Mom find that voice and that power within her?*

Fortunately, after a moment, she nodded. "I understand what you're saying," she said, "I still don't agree with you that it's me; I still think it's him—and he needs medication." But at least she was open to discussing it, and she finally came to the conclusion that there were things that she could do.

That was good enough for me. "What do you lose by trying?" I asked.

As she described it, their nightly homework routine had been going something like this: Josh would work on his math, seem to know how to do it—and then, in the last 20 minutes, become completely lost and be unable to solve problems he'd handled well earlier. It was as though it was all new to him. He was no longer in tune with it, disengaged and tired. He then pushed back.

"It's not that he can't learn," I told her, "or that he's not smart. He's simply telling you *I'm sick and tired. I don't want to do this anymore.* He's honestly telling himself *I can't.* And he's not lying. At that point, he really feels like he *doesn't* know it. He clearly doesn't have a learning problem, since he knew it five minutes ago. There's no medical condition that would give him those symptoms."

So we began talking about a workable strategy. I suggested that she might say, "Okay, we'll close the book now—you'll take the homework back to your teacher, and it will be unfinished. But that's okay. That's all we're going to do tonight."

She would then write an honest note to the teacher: *When we got to this part of the homework, Josh was so tired that he wasn't able to work anymore.* However she phrases it, she should simply write the truth.

Later, after dinner, she would have a conversation with Josh along these lines: "Josh, you were not able to do the amount of work you're reasonably expected to do. And you know what? Mom's also tired, because you struggled more than you needed to with that homework. So you're going to go to bed"—and here she'd look at her watch—"at 8:00 instead of your normal bedtime, 9:00. So at 7:30, I want you on your way to bed."

At this point, Josh will give her a *you've gotta be kidding me* look. *Are you serious about this?*

My instructions to this mom? Say it with all the seriousness in the world. "Of course I'm serious. It's obvious that you need your rest. In fact, you know what? You probably need that extra rest for the rest of the week."

> Develop eyes that see your child's abilities and potential.

Josh's mom interrupted: "I'm supposed to punish him because he wasn't able to finish his homework?"

"You're not punishing him; you're teaching him how to handle himself. You're going to give him the incentive—the strength—to power through his homework, which is an essential life skill. After two or three days of being put to bed while there's still sunlight peeking through his window, he's going to think to himself *I'd better make sure that I stick with it for those five or ten extra minutes and finish the work.*"

That's a consequence that matches the behavior. It's not like taking away his 3DS or his iPod because he didn't do his homework. Josh insisted that he was tired. Fine—he was given more time to sleep. It will not hurt his mom, and it definitely won't hurt him. Give him time to sit and contemplate, letting *him* figure out for himself how to get out of the situation he had helped create.

Not incidentally, Mom is also delivering the message that she's the boss. She's made a decision—one that makes sense—and she'll stick by it.

"Just give it a try," I concluded. "We'll see whether it works or not."

Josh had been sitting there, listening to all this, and now I turned to him. "Josh?"

"Yes, ma'am?"

"How does this sound to you? If your mom does what we're talking about, would you think she was being mean to you?"

"No, ma'am."

"Because you understand that she's only trying to help you get enough rest so that the next day you'll be able to think and do well at school."

He nodded reasonably; it made all the sense in the world in his little brain. "Yes, ma'am. I can see that."

But even more than sleep or medication, Josh needed a strong dose of self-confidence. I said, "You know, I remember that you are a great basketball player. Are you going play basketball this year?"

"I guess so."

"Why do you only *guess so?*"

"Because I don't like basketball so much."

"Wait a minute—you're a fantastic basketball player."

"I like football better, ma'am, but my mom won't let me play."

I looked back over at Mom, who had pursed her lips, and said, "Okay, I understand—you have to live by Mom's rules. If Mom feels that football is dangerous, or she can't get you there, then you have to make do with that. But are you willing to play basketball if Mom can arrange it?"

"Yes. It's just not my favorite."

"Well," I asked turning back to the mom, "can you make sure that he plays basketball?"

"If he doesn't really want to, why should I take the trouble to get him over there?"

"Because he needs it for his self-confidence. The message this young man is getting both at school and at home is that he can't do it—that he's not smart enough, that there's something wrong with him, and that he needs medicine. He needs to go back to remembering that he is really good at something.

> Reaccess your inner voice and intuition. You know your child better than anyone else does!

That something may not be what he likes the most, but he *is* good at basketball: He's good at thinking on the court three steps ahead of the other kids, and he needs to know about himself. He needs that kind of self-confidence.

"Plus, if he's getting more rest, he'll do his homework better, and then his self-confidence will really get a boost. I guarantee it."

With that, she smiled a little. It gave me hope that maybe they could get on the right path to reestablish the bond of affection with her son and help her see what a little champion she had already.

Chapter Eleven

THE RETURN OF THE LITTLE TYRANT

*U*sually, after the initial session, I bring kids and their parents back in four weeks. But because Dan's mom was so concerned about losing control, and because she needed a little pat on the back, I set their next appointment for two weeks later.

So they come in, and she sits down, looking really tense. The first thing she says is: "He's exactly the same. He's no better."

And I think *Oh, no!* I was hoping so much that she'd see at least a little improvement. Even just a glimmer of light at the end of the tunnel would build her self-confidence as a mom.

"Well," I tell her, "it's a process—one step at a time. Maybe it's just too early. But I'm here to help you through this and, if something doesn't work, to help give you some new direction. I'm sure it will work; we just have to persist."

And, of course, I already knew Dan was a tough cookie. But I also had no doubt that it was doable. I'm sometimes reminded in this work of the wild horse that everyone says is impossible to break—until someone figures out how to do it—or of Helen Keller in *The Miracle Worker*, who bit and spat and was totally out of control until her teacher finally uncovered the lovely child underneath. But—horse or child—doing so always takes the whole movie.

At this point, Dan's mom hands me a Vanderbilt form that she filled out before coming in—a numerical assessment of thirty to forty of Dan's specific behaviors. And I look at it, and after a moment, I look back up at her in surprise.

"But according to this, his behavior *is* better. Compared to the one from two weeks ago, it's about *30 percent* better! That's a *huge* improvement!"

What is striking is that she can't see it. She's forgotten how she scored Dan on these assessments last time; she just sees the problems that remain.

> Develop perspective.

"No, no—" I tell her, "this is really *much* better. Let's go over it to see what the differences are."

It turned out that Dan hadn't been having as many tantrums as before, and the ones he did have were far less over the top. And he'd now been in a new daycare for two weeks, which was a real breakthrough. Yes, he was getting some complaints, but he was still there—and that was a first.

"You're not able to see the improvement in that?" I asked.

"I guess," she said, with no enthusiasm at all.

Hmm, I thought. "Listen, you're going to have to do me a favor. You're going to have to develop eyes to see hope and recognize the future your child has. Because until you can see that, you're going to be badly stuck in pessimist land. Only when *your* attitude changes will you be able to smile at him more and will he pay more attention to your words. But you have to see the little bit of good before you can do that."

"I guess," she repeated, in the same tone.

Like so many moms, Dan's mom was simply unable to recognize the degree to which *she* was both the problem and the solution.

We started by working on the new things she'd been doing that had already brought about this improvement. She was being less threatening than she had been before, but at the same time, she was being much firmer. She was making Dan go to bed early, and he was actually doing it; he'd throw just a small tantrum but then pick himself off the floor and go to bed. And he wasn't throwing his food at her anymore when he didn't like it—just crossing his arms and insisting, "I won't eat it!" Which Mom took as failure. "What am I doing wrong?" she wanted to know.

In short, there was a complete absence of perspective; she seemed only to see the negative and was completely unable to recognize progress.

"Okay," I asked, "so what do you do when he does that—refusing to eat?"

"Well, of course, later he's hungry, so I give him something else."

"Excuse me?"

"Well, I can't starve him."

I waited a moment; surely even she had to know how this sounded. But no.

"Listen," I said finally, "you won't be starving him—he has plenty of weight on him. Why not just clearly tell him, 'This is the dinner we made,' and if he still refuses it, put it in Saran wrap and give it to him again tomorrow? By doing this, you would be acting like the boss."

Of course, there's another part to this—something that often makes it so hard for mothers, and especially single mothers, to follow through: They feel tremendous guilt. If there's no father, they feel guilty about that. And if they don't have much money, they feel guilty about that. And their kids quickly learn to manipulate that guilt. The moms are trying to make up for all they think they've put their kids through by being super-nice when in fact what they're doing is warping their kids.

By now it was clear that that's a lot of was what was going on with Dan. Mom was bouncing between fits of screaming and yelling because he wasn't paying attention and guilty bouts during which she gave in to his tantrums and tyrannical demands. She would literally *tell* him, "I know that you don't have a daddy like most of the other kids and that I have to work all day and put you in daycare. I know it's not fair."

The thing is, she put all that into his little brain not by thinking about what was best for him but for her own reasons. It would never even cross his mind that his life was so bad unless she told him so. Why would he even know? It's like comments you often hear from people who lived through the Great Depression: *We didn't even realize we were poor, because no one else had it any better.* And what's the shame in being poor, anyway? Or in being a single mom? That's a matter of circumstances, not a value judgment. Being a good person is something that is rooted in your faith, in your kindness toward others, and in your honor and loyalty—not in how much money you have.

But what happens is that those sorts of life circumstances can become an excuse—not just for the mother but also, very soon, for the child. And once that victim mindset sets in, only bad things follow.

Not that it's only a question of poverty. Middle- and upper-class parents don't have exactly the same problems, but they make just the same mistakes. I remember taking the family of a colleague out to dinner, including their little guy. He was just a little older than Dan, and he acted exactly the same way about food. He ordered one of the most expensive things on the menu, took two bites, and said he didn't want it. It was a bit awkward—since they were my guests—but I said, "John, in our home, we have a rule that unless you eat your food, you will not get dessert. And as my guest, I expect you to follow it. Because after dinner we're going to my home, and we have a really fantastic pie with ice cream waiting for you there—*after* you eat your dinner."

> Don't let children manipulate your feelings of guilt.

"No! I'm not eating it!"

So I didn't push it, and half an hour later we got home, and of course John said, "I want my ice cream and my pie!"

Immediately, his mom stands up, every bit the waitress, goes to the fridge, and comes back with his pie and ice cream.

Naturally, I'm more than a little irritated watching this, with little John eyeing me with a look that says *See? I win!*

So I tell him, "Very nice, John—you got around the Stein family rule."

But of course I'm really aiming my remark at his mom, who gets very flustered. "Oh!" she says, "that's right, Dr. Rose. I forgot."

But by now John is already eating it, with the attitude *Whatever— no one's going to take it away from me now.*

This was the decisive moment. Because she *could* have said, "Sorry—my bad," and taken the pie back, putting it in the freezer. It would have made a powerful impression. Or she could have said, "Does somebody else want this—someone who finished his dinner?" Or, even better, she could have eaten it herself.

> Don't allow your life circumstances to become an excuse. Avoid a victim mindset— both for yourself and for your child.

But there was no chance of that. Why? To her it would have been *mean.*

In fact, it wouldn't have been mean at all but just the opposite; in the grand scheme of things, it would have been a kindness. That's because the results are infinitely better when rules are respected. What's *not* nice is giving your child everything he or she wants. The great writer C. S. Lewis once spoke of "severe mercy," and that's what this is about. It sounds very severe, sitting there eating your kid's apple pie while she cries and screams— it breaks your heart. But to guarantee the best outcome, moms have to show severe mercy.

It's the same kind of love that God has for us. I have no doubt that sometimes, while He's disciplining us, God's heart is breaking. But without that discipline, the consequences would be far more severe. So even though discipline is something we don't like now, ultimately we know that discipline is God's mercy toward us.

Back to Dan's mom. Over and over she kept asking variations on the same question: "What's the secret? What do I do?"

"Okay," I finally said, "the first thing is you're going to have stop with the excuses. You're not a short-order cook. If he goes to bed without dinner, all that happens is he has a lot of time with an empty stomach to figure things out. His little brain will be wondering *How'd I get myself into this situation?*"

"But he's not going to stay in bed—he's going to yell and scream."

"That's okay; it's not the end of the world—he'll just be hoarse the next day. And you'll give him the 'Mom look' and say, 'See? Now you know what happens.'"

But she still refused to get it. She pointed out other ways he had of acting out; she wanted a specific answer for each. "He's been leaning back and tipping his chair and wouldn't listen to me. And finally, yesterday, he leaned back so far that the chair tipped over and he hit his head on the wall, screaming 'I'm hurt, I'm really hurt!'"

> Be consistent and fearless, and bad behaviors will stop. They always do.

"Same answer: 'Now you know.'"

It's almost as if she can't hear, because she just presses on: *He does this to me, he does that to me.*

"Look," I put it to her, "you're just going to have to do this. *You. Are. Going. To. Have. To. Do. This.* Consistently and without fear. And at some point, all these behaviors will stop. How do I know that? Because they always do. Especially at 3 years old. It might take two weeks, or five weeks, but however long it takes, it *will* change."

The truth is, over the years, I've come to realize that there are some moms who, for all their complaints, on some level actually act as if they *want* something to be wrong with their child. Aside from the fact that it absolves them of responsibility, it's almost like they develop an addiction to the drama, the same way certain women can get addicted to an abusive relationship with a man. And having a disaster of a kid gives them an identity; it gives them something to be a martyr about, something to elicit sympathy and pity.

Even well-intended and better adjusted people can fall into the Martyr Mom trap—because, after all, raising a child *is* complicated and hard and frustrating. It's so much easier for them to throw up their hands and say, "It's not my fault! The kid has problems!"

This is the reason there's been such an explosion in medicating children. Today we've got parents running here and there like Paul Revere, shouting, "My child is on the spectrum! My child is on the spectrum!" They tell doctors that their kid has autism or Asperger Syndrome or ADHD—or all of the above. In their view, they just had lousy luck—got a flawed model—and it can't be fixed except by medicine.

And, this being America, when you have that kind of demand, the market responds. So now you've got pharmaceutical representatives constantly in and out of doctors' offices recommending that they prescribe new medicines for their patients, and television commercials everywhere pushing patients to ask for them. So, without question, if parents are intent on their child having a diagnosis, they will get one.

But getting one is not in the child's best interest, and when parents seek a diagnosis as a way of shifting blame, they're limiting their child's potential. Nine times out of ten, if a kid is acting poorly, his or her parents have created this situation, from top to bottom, by using an incorrect recipe for parenting.

> Be very, very careful about labeling your child or pushing for a diagnosis. Kids live up—or down—to expectations.

Unfortunately, a diagnosis will follow the child forever. The unfortunate thing is that unless parents realize that many of these "diagnoses" can also be seen as unhealthy childhood behaviors that can be corrected, their children will suffer as a result. A child will be labeled—and, worse, will label himself. The diagnosis becomes part of the child's identity, part of how he thinks about himself in engineering or math and in social situations. It defines the child. This is what happens when you put a label on someone.

I'll never forget something I was told by a remarkable educator I know. She's about 70 years old now, an old-fashioned kind of educator who gets

Language matters. Messaging speaks.

amazing results. She takes inner-city kids who have median test scores in the 10th percentile and brings them up to around 75th to 80th percentile. How? Through discipline, yes—but also by helping them throw off the labels that have been put on them, persuading them that they're capable of those kinds of results.

I know this from personal experience. Thirty or forty years ago, when I was growing up in New York City, I was in something called the IGC, which stood for "Intellectually Gifted Classes." It was after the Soviet Union had launched Sputnik. These new classes had been started for the students whom America hoped would grow up to challenge the Russians' early dominance in the space race by working for NASA or becoming leaders in other areas. And it worked—because there was such a high level of expectation. Even if we did well, the message was always *We know that you can do better. You're special, you're valuable—you're better. Don't let us down; a lot of money and effort is being invested in you.*

The teachers always used this kind of wording, and knowing we had that kind of potential—and getting that kind of messaging—we responded. *I* responded. I didn't think of it as pressure. It was like *Okay—okay, I get it. A lot is invested in me. A lot is invested in me, so this is what I've got to do.*

But I remember one educator telling me something she'd read about—how one school swapped the intellectually gifted first graders with the ones considered intellectually challenged. Awful as that sounds, that was the kind of experimental stuff they did in New York back then. And guess what happened? Because of the expectations and the language, the kids who were failing started to succeed, and the kids who were succeeding started to fail.

That is an extraordinary piece of information: Language matters. Messaging speaks. Our primary function as humans is how we communicate.

There really is a point where you're choosing whether that child is going to be successful, and it starts by the way you talk to her. Don't label your child. Let your child know you expect a lot of her, and make her buy into your message. Because kids are waiting to find out: *Am I okay? Am I a good person? Do you believe in me?* And they take it from there.

> Speak words of truth with love.

So, again, be very, very careful about pushing for a diagnosis. There's no overstating how damaging it is for children when their misbehavior and tantrums are misinterpreted as an illness. Almost always, the problem is with the parents, who have been taught to abdicate their role as leaders in the life of the family.

In the case of Dan and his mom, as I've continued to see them, little by little she's become more self-assured. She'll usually come in with the same pessimistic *I guess* kind of attitude, and I'll have to get her to think about that. I'll say, "Nope, we have to turn your *I guess* into *I can*, because that's what he needs to see from you. This kid is strong-willed, and has got all kinds of potential. But you should have learned by now: If you don't show your *I can* mentality in front of him, he'll roll right over you."

Chapter Twelve

NIP IT IN THE BUD—BUILDING TOMORROW'S MEN!

Why is it so essential to deal with the bad behavior of a child at the earliest possible moment? Where might a strong-willed child like Dan have been heading if there'd been no intervention—which is to say, without a change in his mom's parenting?

Let's put it this way: When a child's out-of-control behavior is allowed to fester, it *always* gets worse. Watching it progress is like watching a slow-motion train wreck. Failing to correct bad behavior alters the way in which a child's mind develops. The longer these incorrect decision-making pathways are allowed to exist, the harder they will be to alter.

Here is a brief story of two boys—a 9-year-old and a 17-year-old—and their moms. Think of it as a cautionary tale.

The 9-year-old's mom is a family friend—a very, very sweet lady. She's a single mom and has been divorced about five or six years. The boy attends a private school, and he's an excellent student—so that's not the problem.

But some time ago, we spent what was supposed to be a pleasant and relaxing weekend with them, and it became painfully apparent that the mom's life is not her own. Both she and her son were suffering as a result.

> Unless it is stopped and corrected, bad behavior *always* gets worse. Don't assume that it will just go away.

She was continuously giving in to whatever her little guy wants.

His actions went way beyond disrespect. He constantly interrupted her when she spoke, but even that doesn't adequately describe it. When she was saying something, he'd give a belittling snicker, at once challenging and demeaning. If she suggested that they go somewhere for lunch, he'd say, very insolently, "No way—I don't like that place." It was things like that—not huge, but constant and extremely telling. He treated her almost like an annoying sibling rather than as a parent to whom he owed deference and respect. In fact, one of the things he'd do when we were driving in the car was "playfully" intrude on Mom's space, pushing his arm heavily against hers so that she had to push it back. Then he'd do it again—and again. And then, if she was trying to talk with one of the grownups, he'd throw his arm around her.

He constantly had to make himself the focus of her attention, and when he wasn't, he reflexively got unpleasant and aggressive, even to the point of pretending that he was going to punch her—then stopping the punch within an inch of her face.

The mom's reaction? She'd laugh like it was the funniest thing in the world. Or maybe, once or twice, she'd say, "No, no—we don't do that; we don't do that," in the gentlest kind of tone.

As if *No, you don't do that* was about to stop this kid! Clearly, he *did* do that—all the time.

There were obvious boundary and respect issues here, and it made everyone around them uncomfortable.

The whole weekend went on that way. He would bully her into giving him whatever he wanted to eat—or not giving him what he didn't want to eat. He even made her go to bed at the same time when he went to bed. And on two separate occasions, again in the car, he claimed he saw a flea and slapped her arm so hard it left a mark.

That was as much of his bad behavior I could tolerate. I said, "Look, you can't do that! Under no circumstances is a boy supposed to hurt his mom! You're getting stronger and stronger, and this kind of behavior can't go on. You're going to hurt your mom if it continues."

That brought his defiant look—this is not a kid used to being told what to do. But, of course, his mother said nothing.

The next morning, at the breakfast table, when his mom was trying to talk with us, he took her face in his hands and spun it around to face him. Making believe he was just playing, he announced, in a big monster voice, "You will look at me when I'm talking to you."

Once again, I intervened. Spot correcting, I talked to him—but of course I was really addressing her. "Listen," I said, "when you do these kinds of things, and show this kind of disrespect for your mom, it will not stop there.

> Make your message clear: "These are my rules, and this is the way it is here."

Eventually, you will do that with other women. It will harm other people—but, young man, it is also going to harm you. You will become a wife-beater, an abuser—someone who treats other people, and especially women, badly." I was working on the mom, because, as always, she had to be reached before she was able do what was required to reach the child.

And by the end, that, at least, had been achieved. It had been impressed on her that this pattern was intolerable and would continue, and worsen, if not stopped.

Clearly, it won't be easy to change the direction of a child who has gone this far on the wrong path. And it's especially tough for a woman like her, who's on her own. We women are not always as commanding as guys are, and sometimes we give the impression of not having it as together. Plus, there's a good chance that the messaging the boy's getting from her ex-husband, both overtly and covertly, was encouraging his belittling of the mother. For while that can certainly happen when parents are together, and does, obviously it is more likely after an acrimonious split.

But, really, by this point, *how* it happened didn't much matter. The point was to correct it while there was still a chance to break out of this cycle and put the mother–child bond back in equilibrium.

And at least she now was aware of it and was going to try to make it happen. Her son had to be made to hear her saying *No, I may not be perfect, and not all my decisions are going to be right. But I am your mother, and you may not ever belittle my decisions or me. This is going to stop!*

You have to make sure that you message *These are my rules, and this is the way it is here. And I don't care what your dad or other people say. In this home, under this roof, I know everything that I'm supposed to know to raise you. You don't come in here with that lack of respect.*

I told her it was also vital to send the message that niceness does not equate weakness. He had to be made to also hear her saying *Yes, I am nice, and I am polite—I treat other people the right way, and I try to be incredibly loving to you. But do not ever take that for weakness. Mom is strong. I'm strong enough to be kind even when I'm upset—strong enough to be kind even when I disagree with someone. That kind of strength is stronger than yelling.*

The fact is, for all she'd done wrong in the past, as his mom, there was no one better positioned in the world to change her child, no one who could possibly explain as effectively as she could how vital it is that a man treat the women in his life with respect—or describe the consequences when he doesn't.

And to drive the point home to my friend, and everyone else in the same position, I have another story, this one of a 17-year-old. These two boys are similar but are at different stages of life.

The 17-year-old's mom has a lot in common with my friend. Both are single moms, and both are very competent in other aspects of their lives. This woman owns her own business, and she has owned her own business for half of her life, which she manages all by herself, having been more than able to hold her own. In other words, she's exceptionally competent, except in the area that really matters the most—parenting—and in the eyes of her son.

When her son was younger, aged 4, 5, 6, and 7, he was actually a pleasant little boy. He had all kinds of potential. But, like the 9-year-old, he completely dominated his mom. And as he grew up, he became increasingly possessive—and abusive. Now, when he is 17 years old, his mom is very afraid of him, and she's right to be—he's out of

> Another important message: Niceness does *not* equal weakness.

control and can't be reasoned with. This is a kid who could well be headed for very serious trouble.

And at this point, his behavior is so engrained in him that there's no pulling him back, especially by his mom. For all her accomplishments in life, he looks down on her, constantly sneering that she doesn't do anything right.

That's awful for her to have to deal with, and it is a complete lie. But it's not completely unreasonable that he would feel that way. Why? In the role that he's always known her in—that of parent—he's right.

> Respect for women starts in your home.

It's important to remember that as women, we're the safeguards of tomorrow's society. We are guarding the next generation to make sure that men are not abusers of women or of people who have less strength. This respect starts—or stops—with us, in our own homes.

Chapter Thirteen

BUT IT'S
NEVER TOO LATE

*T*here's a woman who came to see me about her third child. She has five children, and loves them to death when they're little. But she told me that they turn into tyrants by the time they're about 7 years old, and then they rule over her life.

It was clear she had great self-confidence issues and found it difficult to be assertive. People had always perceived her as weak, including—*especially* including—her children: and they were right. Nor did it help that her husband was a bully who badmouthed her in front of the kids. Things were so bad that she'd been interned for a time in a state psychiatric unit. Basically, she'd just given up and no longer felt she could parent her kids at all.

By the time I saw her, she already had a couple of disasters on her hands. The first child was a charmer but was very difficult to control.

As a teenager, he began using drugs, and then he began dealing drugs. He ended up in a halfway house and got a girl pregnant at age 17 or 18.

The second boy was even more charming and good-looking than the first. Everybody loved him, but it was obvious from the start that he was heading down the wrong track. He treated the mother with absolutely no respect. She has a heavy accent—which, of course, only added to her insecurity. He would laugh at her whenever she made a mistake. In five minutes, you could see there was a real mean streak in him.

His mother came to see me about her third child, a girl, because it was clear the girl was following the path laid down by her brothers. This child was

> Good parenting starts with a good attitude.

also very dismissive of the mom, saying things like: "You know you really don't know anything, Mom." And this was in front of me!

Yet, for all her deficits, the mom was trying as best she could to recapture her authority. She just didn't know how. Things in her home had been out of control for way too long. This mom asked if she could see me in my behavior clinic, and I was thrilled.

So she and her daughter come into the clinic. I give them an hour for the first appointment, and we start going over all the ways to parent completely differently. It's not a cookie-cutter thing. It's about the parent's attitude. I said, "More than anything else, your kids need a leader. They need for you to speak up and be strong. And even if sometimes you're wrong, it's okay—just hold to it, because they need that firmness and those rules. They need to hear you say *This is the way it's gonna be, and you're just gonna have to live by it.* So now let me tell you what I would do in your place, because it would be completely different."

I told them what I'd do at my home: "When Hannah's sassy and won't listen to me, and I have to tell her something multiple times, there are consequences—and meaningful ones. If I've told her five times to clean her room and have been ignored five times, then she'll get: 'You know what, young lady? You've lost your room for the next three days. You're in a sleeping bag. You're in the hallway.'"

Why that punishment? The room is everything to her; it's her sanctuary. But if she's not acting like a family member, then she won't be treated like one. One time, she refused to help with dinner—so she didn't get dinner. Hannah's now 16 years old, but that doesn't mean she doesn't still have to abide by my rules. If she gets out of control or starts to mouth off, Mom will not get out of control. My world doesn't change because hers does. She has to straighten up and come back into *my* world.

Listening to this, the mom's eyes are getting huge, wanting to hear more. Meanwhile, her daughter, Jennifer, looks stunned. Her attitude is *Are you kidding me? I'm not gonna sleep on a sleeping bag.* In fact, she comes right out and says she'd run away if her mom tried something like that.

"Fine," I said, "that's your problem. But you should think about what's going to happen to you out there alone in the world if you do. Because your mom loves you more than anybody in the whole world, and when you step out that door, you won't find anyone who takes care of you like she does. Certainly not the guys you'll meet—not even the ones that say they love you, or even the ones that think they do. So be very careful what you do."

> Kids need their parent to be a leader—to speak up for them and to be strong.

Before they left, I wrote down a couple of reminders for the mom: She should set and enforce a wake-up time, and chores should be an expectation, not a request.

When they came back four weeks later, Jennifer's still upset with me. She can't believe I'm "making" her mom do these things, and she and her mom are doing a lot of bickering.

I tell her that no, I'm not making her mom do anything; her mom is *choosing* to do these things, and she's right to do so. Jennifer's mom has finally realized that it was time—Jennifer was going down the track of her two brothers.

"Do you like the way they act?" I asked. "Do you like what they're turning into?"

"No."

"Well, you are about to turn into the same thing, and we're going to stop that. Your mom and I are standing in the way of your opening that door—because it's up on the second floor, and there's no porch to step out on. That door only leads down."

She didn't answer—just looked at me.

"Do you want to be like your brothers?"

"No. Of course not. Nobody does."

"What do you want to be?"

"I'd like to be a nurse."

"Down this track that you're heading, you will never accomplish your goals, young lady. Your mom is giving you your future back. It may not be comfortable, and neither she nor I likes doing it, but in the long run, she's giving you the greatest gift she can give."

She sat there a moment, and finally said, "Okay. But I'm still not gonna like it."

That was the beginning. It wasn't easy; there was still plenty of push and pull, and some fighting, but her mom held firm.

After a number of visits, Jennifer comes in with an entirely new attitude.

"Dr. Stein," she says, "I'm getting all A's and B's. I'm not getting into fights in school. And my mom and I aren't fighting anymore, either."

"Oh, my goodness, Jennifer. You don't know how happy you made me."

Then Mom walks in, and she looks like a different person—like the boss. Life is not perfect, but it's so much better.

"Girl," I tell Jennifer, "you will have a future."

It's now a year and a half later. One day recently I came to the clinic, and I find a present all wrapped up. It's a little plaque that they'd bought with their hard-earned money. The words on it describe who a real doctor is: *She's a person who spends the extra moment, and she gives us the time, and she sees the future that I can have instead of the one that others say I should have. My real doctor is a friend.*

It was the sweetest thing, and when I saw Jennifer afterward, I gave her a hug and told her how much it meant to me.

"Well, you know," she said, "I still struggle from day to day. I still want to be the kind of kid that I was. But I understand that for me to do well, I have to live under my mom's rules."

> Consequences for bad behavior have to be real and meaningful.

She's still 14 or 15 years old, and she's got a long way to go. But, without question, she's on her way, headed in the right direction. Her destination is success. And she'll reach it, because her mom finally learned how to lay down the tracks.

There are a number of truisms—I call them the "old granny phrases"—that have now fallen out of fashion: *You made your bed—now lie in it. You're just going to have to stew in your own juices.* While to modern ears they may sound mean, they carry tremendous wisdom. Kids do have to learn the consequences of their behavior—and moms, we have to stand back and let them learn their lessons. But by the same token, we have to be aware of the consequences of *our* behavior for our children.

Chapter Fourteen

THE
LONG GAME

*T*o put it plainly, most of us truly don't understand the extent of our influence on our children's lives. Whether we want to or not, even when it doesn't seem possible—in fact, especially at such times—we have to keep it together for our children.

When our lives unravel, we take our kids with us. Small things can play into the mind of a child in ways that we adults are not even aware of. And some of those things can be life-defining moments.

One such moment that I remember happened when I was a teenager. My mother loved Julio Iglesias, and he came to Santo Domingo for a concert. We arrived very early and were able to get to the front for two excellent seats. It was my job to hold our seats while my mother got us two soft drinks. While she was gone, two older women decided that they deserved to have the two seats that I was holding and tried to shove me out of our seats. I was stuck. I could not be disrespectful to two senior citizens, but I could not lose the seats that my mother had waited so long to get. When my mother returned, these two *spicy pasteles* were still giving me a hard time. Explaining to them how long we had waited in line to get those seats had no effect. Suddenly, and out of the blue, one of the older ladies shoved me down and told me that I did not deserve to have such good seats. Walking down the isle, my mom witnessed the whole thing. When the woman shoved me, Mom bounded down the aisle like the Incredible Hulk. When she reached my side, she reached out with one hand and lifted the woman by the collar. "Keep your hands off my daughter—or else!" she bellowed. This woman realized that she had awakened the wrong mama bear—that my mother was not pleased to see her cub in danger. My mom grew to about ten feet tall that day in the eyes of her daughter.

> The long game means that even when your world is chaotic—*especially* then—you have to parent deliberately and consciously.

No one's perfect. We all have rough days, times when we fall apart or collapse with fatigue and feel like we can't get back up again. I certainly have days like that myself. I have a business to take care of and responsibilities to other people's kids, and sometimes when I get home, I'm absolutely spent. But those are the times when understanding the long game is most crucial. Instead of snapping at your kid, you say, "You know, I don't have time for this right now. Let me get my head together. Go and read a book, and we'll talk later."

The long game means that even when the world is chaotic, you have to be conscious of parenting deliberately. Life happens, and no one is immune to life. So maybe during those down times, when you're upset or overwhelmed, you won't parent quite as well as you'd like. But what's key is perseverance—knowing what your goals are and sticking with them. Because your kids are always watching you and your behavior.

> Perseverance is key:
> Know your goals and
> stick with them.

Obviously, there are different kinds of chaos, and some are easier to overcome than others. While every parent goes through ups and downs, sometimes the downs are very deep valleys. All of a sudden, you're bankrupt, or your home's foreclosed on, or your husband of fifteen or twenty years leaves you. Suddenly, you have to be both the mom and the dad and also the breadwinner.

No one minimizes any of that. Yet it is at precisely the times when things are bleakest that we most need to keep playing the long game. Even if it feels like everything is coming apart, you cannot surrender. Even if you feel like you're doing poorly at not just life but also parenting, set a goal of improving half a percent each day. In other words, pull yourself out of it—do one thing half a percent better than you did yesterday. Make those small, incremental changes, and in seven months, you will have improved 100 percent.

If you're parenting deliberately, with love and with a vision, over the long run, there's going to be a positive outcome for your child and for your family. Putting your values and principles into your child ensures that he or she will have a future. But if you're parenting unconsciously, without thinking about the long game, your lasting influence on your child will be very small. The consequences will be devastating for your child and his or her future success in life.

Years ago, I had a friend who had a child the same age as my daughter Hannah. The mom had all these symptom-based problems that nobody could diagnose and was generally just overwrought and depressed. Finally she just threw in the towel and said, "I can't work. I can't, I can't—I can't." Her disability insurance kicked in at that time and gave her enough to pay the bills and scrape by. So she stayed home in her nice little house and did nothing.

> It is vital for parents to understand the depth and extent of their influence on their kids.

Her attitude was that it was no big deal: So what if her child saw her moping around the house? I wanted to go over there and shake her, saying: "You can't do this to your child— you're gonna bring your kid down with you!"

Of course, her daughter suffered. And it got more and more apparent as she grew older. This young teenager, Serenity, has now attempted suicide several times. She's been admitted to psychiatric units. She's been diagnosed as a "cutter."

This child had such possibilities. But now she's dysfunctional, because her mom was dysfunctional. The child's friends did all they could. They worked with her constantly, thinking they had to save her, but by then the damage had been done.

There's a term I like to use: the "circle of damage." When we drop the parenting ball, that ball is a like a bomb. When it hits the ground, it explodes and creates a field of debris around us. Our kids are the ones standing closest, and they become collateral damage. They cannot escape the blast zone.

Sure, there will always be a few kids who beat the odds, who succeed despite their parents. But even in

> Your actions, habits, and behaviors will shape your child.

most of those cases, if you look closely enough, they will have found surrogate parents—relatives, teachers, coaches, or friends who stepped in to fill a parenting vacancy.

> Like an athlete in training, you require time and perseverance to build good parenting skills and muscles.

I can't say it enough: It is vital for a mom to understand the depth of her influence and to have a constant awareness of that influence. Your actions, habits, and behaviors shape your child. When you're doing things right, you should be aware of it—but, even more important, be aware when you're doing things wrong.

Building up that rigorous approach to parenting is not unlike the way an athlete builds up to the giant slalom or running hurdles. It takes time and perseverance to build up those skills and those muscles, and you won't do it perfectly at the start.

But parenting is the most important race you'll ever run. It's a long-distance race, and you can never lose sight of the consequences of losing.

Chapter Fifteen

GIVE YOURSELF
A BREAK

While by now it should be clear that I never stop stressing the extent of a parent's influence on his or her child, it is also important to note that even that influence has its limits. So parents also have to know how, and when, to give themselves a break.

Quite simply, being deliberate as a parent is not the same as being all-knowing. Parenting is an incredible undertaking, and if you dwell too much on what you think you're doing wrong, you can turn yourself into a nervous wreck.

Even if you get your parent-centered life working properly, not everything will be in your hands. There will always be things you won't understand or be able to change about your child, no matter how hard you try—because in the end, in crucial ways, each child is his or her own person.

A friend of mine asked me to lunch recently to talk about her son. This woman had understood the depth and the wealth of the responsibility that she had as a parent from the beginning. This was someone who researched child-rearing like crazy—who went out and bought all those parenting books, who understood that children need to laugh, who understood that children need to be read to, and who had done what she thought was right every step of the way.

> No parent is all-knowing. There's no perfect formula for raising children that works every time, for every child.

For all that, she didn't get the kind of child she expected. Her son grew up very stoic and emotionless, even a little robotic. This is not the way either she or her husband is at all, and it was killing her. Why wasn't their child more like them?

By the time he was a teenager, Mom was beating herself up more than ever and desperately trying to change him. "What did I do?" she kept asking. "What did I do? How did he get this way?" She blamed herself.

Well, naturally, she got the answers she was looking for. One friend told her that it sounded like he had Asperger Syndrome. Somebody else told her he has a brain imbalance. She took him for various tests and finally took him to therapy.

The truth? He's just his own kid, and he happens to be different from the parents. He is more self-contained, less emotional, and less demonstrative. He is *different from his parents*—but there is nothing wrong with him.

Some kids simply are their own people. You see families in which everything works just as the parents hope and expect—for one child. Whatever parenting Mom and Dad do, that child is just golden. Then the next child comes along, and it's hard to believe he or she is from the same parents—and the parents immediately blame themselves.

It's almost as if parents think that there's a perfect formula, that everything is dependent on them—*I didn't give that child enough mommy time, or I didn't read enough to that one.*

But that's completely unrealistic. We're only human, and each of our kids is unique. It would be unnatural if in some ways we didn't treat them differently. Our behavior has to be tailored to each child. But—something to always bear in mind—our parenting treatment of the child doesn't have to be equal to be fair.

So now my friend's son is 19 years old and in college, and he's happy, with his own circle of friends. Yet the mother is *still* beating herself up because he's not who she wanted him to be.

Why? In the end, no matter what, children are their own people. Kids are completely unique. This boy is wonderfully and beautifully made, created by the Lord to be the person he's supposed to be. And he was just meant to be this kind of strong, stoic boy. This mom needed to be freed to enjoy the fruit of her work. Her son is a good young man worthy of going forward into the next generation! Most important, as a mom, she should be proud of her work.

But, for all that, her parenting made a *huge* difference. If she hadn't done all of the exceptional work she did, he might well have ended up lacking morality and

In the end, each child is his or her own person; not everything is in your hands.

not having the tools that he needed to succeed in life. When I told her this over lunch, she started crying.

"What's wrong?" I asked. "Did I say something bad?"

She just looked at me. "It's just always been such a weight on my shoulders all my life. I just thought I was a crummy mom, and I wasn't able to give him the nurturing and the things that he needed so that he would become the sort of young man and human being I hoped for."

> We're all works in progress. Each of us, as we mature throughout life, has a story to share with the next generation.

This is the second woman who has approached me this way. The other had a child who had autistic tendencies, and she started telling me about all the things she'd done and all the therapies she'd tried.

"He's in his twenties," she said, "and he still struggles."

"Does he live on his own?"

"Yes, he does."

It turned out he had completed two years of college and had decided that college wasn't what he wanted to do. He's pretty successful at a lot of things. Sure, he has trouble with some things involving organization or follow through, and sometimes his mom comes over to help him think things through, but generally, he's doing fine.

"Listen," I said, "he's still a work in progress. But you know what? We're all works in progress. What you don't realize is that through your parenting, you saved his life. You gave him hope and a future. Imagine if you'd done nothing. Who would he be today if you'd done nothing?"

It could be that some of what she did along the way sounded like nagging. But what she was doing, really, was helping him be a person who would fit well into society.

She had the same reaction—that of a weight lifting from her shoulders. It was such a revelation to this mom—that she had changed the trajectory of her child's life forever.

Chapter Sixteen

THE HEALTHY HOME— HOW DO WE BUILD IT?

*W*hat does a successful home look like? It is one in which the parent–child dynamic is in balance, in which the parent is the boss and the child understands that there are rules to be followed. The goal is to implant in the child's brain an understanding that, though he may disagree with the person in control, that person always has his best interests at heart. In setting down these rules, the parent is doing more than just creating harmony in the short term; he or she is laying down a set of tracks that the child can follow to become his best, most successful self.

Of course, the question so many parents have is *How do I make that happen?*

Indeed, some can no longer even imagine that such a thing is possible.

Here, then, are my suggestions for what is involved in establishing a healthy home, arranged by the age of your child.

NEWBORNS

Job number one is getting your child to sleep on a regular schedule, including through the night. Doing that not only preserves household sanity but also begins establishing a set of routines that work for everyone.

As an expectant mother, I knew how vital this would be, since in the months before my daughter arrived, I was about to open my pediatric practice. Fortunately, just at that time, I found *On Becoming Baby Wise*, a book by Gary Ezzo and Dr. Robert Bucknan that was extremely helpful to me.

Among other things, the authors laid out a plan to have children sleep through the night at six weeks. My husband scoffed at that, saying that it was impossible, but I set to work implementing their plan.

Generally, when a newborn falls asleep, we're grateful; the last thing we want to do is wake him or her—after all, that time is manna from heaven for us. That's completely understandable, but according to this plan, it is completely wrong. I wouldn't let Hannah nap more than an hour or two, and when I gently roused her from her sleep, I was sure to be prepared for everything that needed to happen next—feeding her, talking to her, playing with her—so that in a very little while, waking her began to feel like a routine to both of us.

Pretty soon, in the evening, she would almost fall asleep before the end of her bath, with the water warm and lullabies playing in the background. It was almost as if I were hypnotizing her into falling asleep.

In those early weeks, she'd wake up during the night—first at 2 a.m., then at 3 a.m.—a little bit later each week. I would pick her up without saying a word, feed her, burp her, and put her right back to sleep. Gentle—but short and sweet. I wanted her to understand that this was not mommy time; it was feeding time—short and sweet.

Sure enough, one morning, when she was four weeks old, she was sleeping until 6:00 a.m. By five weeks and six days, I woke up at 6:00 a.m. after having put her down at 9:00 p.m. and said, "Oh, my Godness—she slept through the night!" It happened just like the book said. I still chuckle when I tell this story, because I remember my husband saying that it couldn't be done.

Based on my own experience with Hannah, I have incorporated that wisdom into my practice. In the same way, it is important to very quickly start centering feeding, changing, and nap times around Mom's schedule. Again, the longer you wait, the harder it will be. Say you've got a 1-year old who's still not sleeping through the night—by now, the entire household revolves around trying to get her to sleep. When the child finally goes to sleep, at 8:30 or 9:00 p.m., the parents are exhausted. Even then, they are still unable to relax—because their child will be up again at 11:00 p.m. And it's hardest on the mom— she's unfulfilled as a mother, a wife, and a person, because nothing is working and everyone is frustrated. The home becomes a place of unhappiness and stress for everyone.

So it's vital to start setting a schedule by limiting nap times during the day, with Mom envisioning how she wants her day to be arranged, allowing her time when she's not totally occupied with the baby.

I know that for many who've been through the wringer with very young children, that sounds like an impossibility. In fact, it's completely doable—it just takes willpower and stick-to-itiveness.

Solid foods come in somewhere between 4 and 8 months of age, and by the time the child is 9 to 12 months old, he or she should be on a regular feeding pattern, eating three times a day. Ad hoc feeding is not good for the baby's brain, because it puts on the child the responsibility of prompting Mom rather than the other way around. It leads to chaos in the life of the mother and the child.

The other key thing at this very early age is making sure you're stimulating the child verbally—having good mommy–child time by talking to him or her. This involves not only how often but also in what ways Mom speaks to her child. *Tone of voice* is very important. So many parents talk to their little ones in a sing-song or in a voice that's high-pitched and childlike, often imploring or asking permission from the child. You hear it all the time at the mall: "Would you be a good girl for Mommy so Mommy can talk to the lady?" If we grown-ups can't stand that voice, just imagine what that does to a brain in the process of being formed! Moms must learn again to speak to their child with their mom voice—one that is firm, directing, and loving.

A word I repeat all the time is *deliberate*. How would you like your schedule to be? How would you like your child to feed? Answer those questions for yourself, then deliberately arrange life in your household accordingly. These are the building blocks that form the foundation for healthy childhood. Good moms are proactive.

Tips for Newborns

- Newborns can—and should—sleep through the night by 6 to 8 weeks of age.

- Set up a daily schedule that works for you—and stick to it.

- From the beginning, make sure you're stimulating your baby verbally.

AGES 2 TO 5

Toilet training is another area where it's important to be proactive.

I remember, before I became a mother myself, hearing older black moms say that they had toilet-trained their kids by the time each child turned 1 year old, and I remember how hard I found it to believe. I figured *Well, maybe 18 months—maaaaybe.*

But by the time Hannah was 18 months old, I'd had enough of changing diapers. Since it took a while to get my practice going, it was necessary for me to be frugal at home. To save money, I was the last mother in America with her child still in cloth diapers. This was a great motivator for me to get Hannah toilet-trained. No one likes to clean cloth diapers. By now everything else was on target— her sleeping and feeding schedules were just as I wanted them—so I decided to also give her a set potty time. Every two to two-and-a-half hours, I took her to the toilet and established a routine for her. And, sure enough, that child was potty-trained between 18 and 22 months.

This is a huge deal for a child—a real developmental leap— because being able to control your bodily functions is paramount in brain development. Delaying this key milestone will delay those that follow it.

When moms are skeptical about the timing, I put it to them this way: puppies know when to go by 6 or 8 weeks old, and 18 to 20 months is just the human equivalent.

Then we come to another key rule in the parenting of toddlers: the word *no.* Not only do little ones not hear that essential word as much as they used to, but also a fair numbers of parents actually take pride in *never* exposing their child to it! It is not healthy for the child's developing brain to have no limits or boundaries. It sets the brain on a completely different pathway that is not in their best interest. I see the results in my office all the time—2- and 3- and 4-year-olds who have had so little exposure to any kind of authority figure that they're literally dumbfounded when, in me, they're confronted with one.

Indeed, 90 percent of the time, when I walk in and give such a child that in-control look, I'll immediately own the room. "You're going to have to be very quiet," I say to one of these children, "because your mom and I have to talk. Do you understand that?" And the look I get says it all: *Wow, I've never seen this before. What is this about?* By then the parents will have already completely surrendered their power. Many parents today think that a child that is poorly behaved is normal, since nearly all of today's children are poorly behaved. This, of course, is not true. We have traveled that far off the path of good parenting.

Typically in such a situation, the child will quickly begin to try manipulating the mother. He or she might cry a little and bury his or her head in Mom's lap, then turn around and look up at me to see what's going to happen.

I'll say something like: "Mom, just put her in that chair next to you." Then, locking eyes on the child: "This is your time to be a big girl. Do you think you could do that for the doctor?" I look directly at her and say: "Good." It is essential to understand that the tone that I use when talking to these children is a commanding tone—not a pleading tone. When the child follows my direction, the parent is nearly always amazed. I usually get a "that never happens in my home—I could sure use you around the house" type of comment. I like to remind these moms that I am *not* a "child whisperer." Every mother can learn to talk to her child in an authoritative tone and get the same results.

Almost every time, that is all that is necessary. It's amazing how ready children are to accept authority! They crave it, because they don't *want* to control their homes. It is far too stressful. Relinquishing control makes their lives so much simpler.

And, of course, the parents' lives are immeasurably easier, too.

How does it work?

Heading out to the store with her 2-year-old, an authoritative mom will be proactive. She locks eyes with the child as she's buckling him into the car seat and lays down the ground rules: "You are not going to ask for anything, and you are not going to have a tantrum." The child may not like it, may fidget a bit, and may not want to assent, but once he has verbalized agreement—"Yes, Mommy"—the child understands that such an agreement constitutes a pact, and he will live by it.

It's amazing how many parents don't understand that.

Can a mother become an authority figure after having gotten off on the wrong foot? Of course—though whether it happens, and how quickly, obviously depends on the age of the child. With a 2-year-old, it can generally be accomplished within a few weeks if—and this is a huge if—Mom masters her new role of authority figure and plays it consistently. It has to be expressed in her tone of voice and physical appearance. It is her ability to say, with absolute conviction, "No, you do *not* behave that way" and, if the child persists, to follow through with consequences that will change the dynamics of the mother–child relationship for the better.

What kind of consequences? Again, it depends on a vast range of variables, starting with the child's age and the nature of the misbehavior. Say, in the example above, that the child ends up breaking the pact and having one of those really egregious, over-the-top temper tantrums in the middle of Walmart. The mom would put the child under her arm—in what I call the airplane maneuver—turn around, march him out of the store, and go home. Once the child has calmed down, they have the conversation—which, at that age, is very simple. No threats—because they have no concept of that—just completely concrete consequences. If there's a ritual of an after-dinner cookie, it might be "You behaved very badly, and I was so embarrassed by the way you acted in the store, that you will not get a treat today. But you will get it tomorrow when you're well behaved again." And if *that* launches a tantrum? "Uh-unh—no more of that."

Of course, there's the other possible reaction: the one where the child looks at you with those pitiful puppy-dog eyes that make you want to run over and give him the biggest hug in the world. The child is heartbroken at these moments, and so is the mother. So was *I* as a mom—and I understand that this is the hardest part of all. But it's essential to refrain from giving your child that hug, because this is *not* the moment to show them how easily they're able to break your heart. In refraining, you are loving. You're setting that baby's brain straight by doing that.

Much better to say: "So you are going to bed early tonight, because you need your time to think."

Even as you reassure with absolute love and give your child a kiss as you put her down, there can be no compromises about bad behavior. Even a 2-year old understands that. The fact is, at that age, children are Silly Putty, easy to mold back into the proper form. They might cry themselves to sleep (and you might come back in and reassure them)—but that's okay. That kid has run up against the wall of Mom's authority—and in letting him or her do so, Mom is making sure that her child will avoid running into much harder and more unforgiving walls later in life.

Of course, little ones also delight in being family helpers, and at right around 2 years, moms and dads should harness their children's goodwill and have them start pitching in. Doing so makes them feel important and secure. When you don't harness a child's desire to be useful early on, instead waiting until they're older, they'll feel like you're imposing on them rather than that the family is working as a team.

Again, it's important to be proactive and very clear, giving your child only tasks for which he or she is developmentally equipped. As parents, it is our job to match our children's level of development to what they are able to do capably and well for themselves.

When gardening together, a parent might say: "I need you to throw this away, then come back here." After dinner: "I need you to clear just this and this off the table."

Structure, discipline, and authority—these are the world's best investments. By age 5, every child should be able to follow instructions, behave with respect, and have self-control. We're either going to invest early in our children, or you'll have to put in a lot more work at the end of their childhood—with a much smaller return.

Tips for Toddlers

- Be proactive with toilet training. Not only is it a real developmental leap, but being able to control bodily functions is key in brain development.

- *No* is not a bad word for toddlers to hear. Children crave authority—they don't want to be in control.

- There can be no compromises with bad behavior.

- Harness a child's natural desire to help. Give your child appropriate, regular tasks, and let him or her know that he or she is part of the family team.

AGES 5 TO 12

Good parenting is constant, with the long view always in mind. The sense of responsibility and personal accountability that parents begin nurturing in very young children must continue to grow at the same pace they do. No child of 5 or 8 or 10 years old should ever hear the word "chores" and respond *Huh?*

A child's respect for the adult figures in his life involves the child's understanding what his own responsibilities are. A parent shouldn't have to tell a child every time to clean up his room, to fold the laundry, or to take out the trash, and the child shouldn't expect praise for doing so. If a child has been raised properly, it should be understood that helping out with chores is simply expected from members of the family.

Yet when I bring up the subject of chores with moms and dads in the office, over and over I hear some variation on *They clean up their room*—as if that should be enough. No, it's not. That's not a chore, it's a basic responsibility—and it's usually done minimally, anyway.

Sometimes I even hear *Well, they do their homework.*

It's amazing how little is expected of children in so many homes these days. When my mother was 8 or 9 years old, she was expected to kill a chicken, pluck the feathers, and get it ready to cook. Every child she knew did the same, and many kids in the United States had equivalent tasks—tasks that we now we think of as adult responsibilities.

One obvious result, as we've discussed before, is spoiled and entitled children. But another is overworked, distressed, and exhausted moms, who feel like they're carrying the burdens of the whole household—because they are.

So that rule is pretty basic: Give kids chores! It will help their self-confidence to know that they are part of the family team. Remember, chores are not for your benefit at the beginning; they are for your child's.

My other key piece of advice for parents of children in the middle years might also sound obvious: Talk with them regularly and openly, sharing your thoughts, your values, and your faith. Yet it's astounding in how many homes that just does not happen.

Dinners, in particular, should be a safe haven of family time for children. No television in the background, no tablets, mobile phones off—a free back-and-forth discussion of the day's events with an emphasis on the children carefully listening to what Mom and Dad have to say. When parents neglect to build that relationship when a child is 8 or 9 years old, still so innocent and accepting, it's infinitely harder to retrieve later on.

At those ages, kids always have a lot on their minds—something their teacher said, trouble they're having with some other kid, or something they may have heard about in the news. Those are the moments for parents to listen and respond with their own perspective on the world. This is an excellent time for parents to instruct and teach their child. You're not going to back them up when they're doing something wrong, but you'll always give solid advice.

Almost no subject should be off the table, not even those that might be a little uncomfortable or embarrassing, because you're setting a precedent. Later on, in the teen years, when the child usually has far more difficult questions, it is essential that he or she know that

Mom and Dad are the ones to go to for the right answers. That just won't happen at 13 or 14 years old if the foundation is not laid down early on in their family life.

Incidentally, do not hesitate to freely share things about yourself and your own childhood—including mistakes you made—as your way of letting your children know you were a kid also, far from perfect. It's amazing how many doors that can open. When you share those moments, you're not only giving your child a heritage, you're letting him see that you're human. It's an opportunity to talk not only about times you felt wronged as a child but how you handled it. And in pointing out the ways you did things wrong, and explaining what you should have done instead, you can actually turn your mistakes into a learning experience for your child. Now, hopefully, when they make mistakes, at least they'll be *different* ones.

The fact is, a child who hears from even one adult whom he or she trusts about the dangers of drugs is something like 40 percent *less* likely to engage in that sort of risky behavior.

One last thing—there are probably a lot of you, reading that part about turning off the television at dinner time and setting aside mobile phones and tablets, who rolled your eyes and said to yourselves *Right—fat chance*. Well, for the record, I'll say it again here: These electronic devices have come to play far too dominant a role in the lives of our children and our families.

So there can be no negotiation when the parents lay down the law in this regard. Parents must not allow the children the *Just fifteen more minutes!* or *Until it's over* that infringe on important family time. Doing so sends the message that the child has power in this situation. Once you've set limits, that must be the way it is.

I advise that children of this age be allowed to use electronic and digital devices, not including for homework, for no longer than one hour on weekdays and two hours on weekends. *Listen,* I tell parents, *I know how hard it is to do this. I know it's going to be a struggle. But you've got to protect your child's brain!* This is especially important for the younger children. We have all seen 2- to 5-year-olds playing endlessly on their tablets. These kids begin to develop relationships with the characters in the games that they play. They have a very difficult time differentiating the real world from the tablet world. These children, if left alone in that world, will have increasing difficulty establishing real-world relationships as they get older.

Tips for 5- to 12-Year-Olds

- Give kids chores!

- Talk to your children regularly and share your thoughts, values, and faith.

- Make dinner family time—no television, tablets, or mobile phones.

- Limit use of electronic devices to no longer than an hour on weekdays.

TEENAGERS

Modern adolescence is a subject so vast and complex that it couldn't be covered by an entire library, let alone in a brief section of a single book. But, once again, I want to hit on a few key points that have been especially useful in dealing with teens and their parents in my practice. (And, hardly incidentally, I am the mother of a teen myself!)

I think it was Shakespeare who said that if we could skip the ages from 13 to 23, there would be no folly in the world. Teenagers make *bad* decisions. That's the hallmark of a still-growing brain. Though they can be as large and strong as adults, their decision-making tree is still very short and has few branches. So they'll often do things that, if they bothered to think about it, even they should know are dumb. Ask them afterward why they did it, and what you get is a blank stare and *I don't know.* Some parents think that these children are just being difficult or are trying to hide the real reason they did something. It is important for parents to understand that these children truly don't know why they made these bad choices. Their brain has not yet developed the capability to answer the question *Why?*

So it's our job as parents of teens—our *number-one job*—to preempt that and prevent as many of these bad decisions as we can by training our children how to think and make decisions.

Moms, especially, are very intuitive, and there's no substitute for their gut feeling that their child might be in jeopardy. So I preach that when someone has that feeling, she should respect it. While we obviously can't protect our children from everything, there are certain situations and people that we must be certain our kid steers clear of. This concerned mom should start by having a serious conversation with the child, because usually the child has been trying to tell you something. That is why Mom has that gnawing mom feeling.

Sure, maybe you're helicoptering, maybe you're overreacting—but far, far, far better to err on the side of prudence.

Should we be spying on our adolescent children, reading their text messages or raiding their underwear drawers? Sadly, in today's work, that question is entirely reasonable, and there are times I would recommend it. Obviously, if you've established the parameters of personal responsibility and accountability from the beginning, along with the understanding of the consequences that will ensue if that trust is ever violated, it is far less likely that you'll ever have to "spy."

Still, in parenting almost more than in anything else, the best medicine is always preventive. If a parent has so much as an inkling of a suspicion that something is amiss, she should not hesitate to pick up that kid's mobile phone and have a very close look.

The fact is, in the age of sexting, you're protecting not just their minds but their hearts and character. The images our kids are exposed to these days can be damaging not only in the short term but also, in some cases, forever.

This leads, inevitably, to the subjects of dating and sex. Frankly, if a parent is waiting to have this conversation in the teen years, he or she is way too late; it should have happened around age 10 or 11.

My personal view, based on everything I've seen? At least through the high school years, teenagers should not engage in sex. Difficult as that message is to put across in today's America, I believe parents should make their feelings about this clear from the beginning—because there are real potential consequences for the child's future, especially for a girl. Beyond the very real potential for pregnancy and significant sexually transmitted diseases, there are the severe emotional costs that can come from such an intense relationship even for those emotionally prepared for it. It is another way in which today's children are growing up way too quickly—without, in many important ways, having grown up at all. Moreover, all the statistics show that early sexual activity is linked with other kinds of poor decision making, like doing drugs, drinking, and driving under the influence.

In my view, it's simply infinitely wiser and more prudent to not walk through that door. It is in your child's best interest to steer clear of these problems until he or she is emotionally and mentally able to deal with the decision making and its consequences.

Tips for Teenagers

- Teenagers make bad decisions—that's the hallmark of a still-growing brain.

- The best medicine is preventive. If you even *think* something is amiss, don't hesitate to act.

- Have the conversation about sex and dating *before* your child hits puberty.

Chapter Seventeen

HOLDING
YOUR GROUND

*T*here is terrific peer pressure on parents these days—not just from other parents but sometimes also from teachers and society at large. It is pressure to do things the way that others are doing them rather than doing what, in their gut, parents know is right.

That battle must be fought and won, with Mom understanding early on and with absolute certainty how vital it is, when it comes to raising a human being, to stick with the mind over the heart.

This is an especially difficult battle for women, because by our nature, we're swayed by our hearts and our emotions. This is something our child intuitively understands and unknowingly uses against us. But that only means we have to be all the more conscious in our parenting.

Peer pressure these days can be nothing short of noxious. It was a lot easier when I was growing up, thirty and forty years ago, because parents were almost always on the same page. If you happened to wear a skirt that was too short or say a bad word in the street, somehow, before you got home, your mom always knew. It was as if there was just this extraordinary cabal of moms, a consortium of parents, all working together, looking out for their own kids' futures by making sure the kids around them were all growing up walking a straight line.

Heck, I'd even get ratted out for my table manners! Back then, mothers took corrective actions decisively. When my mother was told that my manners were not those of a young lady, I was immediately enrolled in etiquette classes.

Much as we sometimes chafed under this system, it was immensely reassuring for us kids. It made us feel secure knowing that wiser heads were in charge, looking out for us.

There was also among those parents a sense of shared morality. *They* knew right from wrong, and they didn't hesitate to let you know which was which:

> Examine your own motivations: *Is this serving my child's needs, or mine?*

Being "judgmental" was not yet considered a sin. So you certainly wouldn't have that one kid in the neighborhood who was allowed to read pornography at home, to smoke cigarettes, or to smoke dope with his dad on weekends. Due to the efforts of all moms working together to raise good citizens, a child who broke all the rules was a rare bird.

Today, in an era when moms hesitate to correct their own kids, let alone anyone else's, peer pressure is different. In many cases, it means conforming to not only different norms but also worse ones.

This definitely applies to the expectations we place on our kids. My Hannah is just an okay student, and I've always encouraged, and sometimes admonished, her to put in more effort—because it's about the effort, not the grades. In my view, "just enough" is not enough; I am challenging her to excel. I know my kid, and I won't be one of those parents who say everything is hunky-dory when it isn't. I look to build her self-confidence rather than her self-esteem.

So I was pretty taken aback when she was in fourth grade and an administrator in her school reprimanded me by saying: "Don't expect her to be perfect—are you perfect?"

> Pick your child's activities wisely. An activity should be a growth experience.

What she was saying, in effect, was that I was making my child anxious and nervous. Few other parents were that demanding and she wanted me to go with the flow.

And, I must admit, it gave me pause. I wondered: *Am I really so mean? Might I actually be causing my 9-year-old daughter mental health issues?*

I was forced to second-guess myself, and I'm a *professional* in the field!

This is the terrible power of peer pressure—it readily makes you question your own instincts. This new peer pressure on Mom is pulling mothers away from parent-centered parenting and into the world of child-centered parenting. And that's a problem: It's causing moms to raise a generation of high-esteem children.

It didn't help when Hannah weighed in—for, of course, a child can always smell weakness. Parroting what she'd heard, she told me she was worried about all the pressure she was under and how it would affect her.

But by then, my head was already back on straight. "That's not going to happen," I reassured her. "You're just doing what kids do, trying to get out of doing something hard."

"Oh, okay," she said, and I haven't heard a word from her about it since.

Talking to other moms and to teachers, hearing what they have to say on child raising, is certainly not a bad thing. But caving into others' views when it means stifling your own voice? That's when it gets dangerous.

Whether you are a mom of limited means or one who is in a position to give your child absolutely everything, you must sometimes fight the overwhelming need to fit in with other moms' parenting. It can be extremely difficult, but you owe it to your child.

Peer pressure presents itself in all kinds of ways. One of the biggest involves the activities parents get their kids into. Many moms rarely consider whether they're pushing a child toward some activity because it's the right thing for the child or whether they're just in competition with other parents and their kids.

Ideally, rather than letting their children take every activity that's momentarily fashionable—soccer, karate, drawing, gymnastics, little league, or horseback riding, or all of them at once—a parent should know intuitively what his or her child does well. Rather than being influenced by other parents, much less letting the child make the decision, firmly guide your child toward the choices that best match his or her talents.

Yet precious few parents grasp this or have the insight to honestly examine their own motivations. If parents were more conscious, they would ask themselves *How does this activity benefit my child? Why am I putting him or her in this class? Will it help my child grow and become better? Does it really speak to his or her talents and answer his or her needs?*

What happens instead, and happens far too often, is that a mom will think *I've got to put my kid in soccer—all the other moms do, and I want him to have friends.* Or *My child is so pretty, she should be a ballerina. I'm putting her in ballet.* Never mind

> Peer pressure from other adults can make you question your own instincts. Don't go wobbly!

that her child might be completely ill suited for team sports or that ballet is meant only for those who thrive on discipline and formalized perfection. Pushing the kid in the wrong direction—especially if it mainly serves the parent's desire to impress other parents—only piles on the stress.

Every child has only so much time between kindergarten and the last day of his senior year of high school, and the choices his parents make about which activities to pursue will impact that child for the rest of his life. Some of those choices could end up being part of the child's profession. But all of the choices will impact, in one way or another, that child's development. So if a child is sacrificing significant time to do something, it should be a growth experience, aimed at truly lifting that child up and guiding him in life as he goes along.

Then, as I've touched on earlier, there is the matter of electronics—mobile phones, tablets, video games, and all the rest—and how much access to them a parent should permit his kids.

Obviously, in many homes this is a battleground between children and their parents, with far too many parents being hesitant to set, and stick to, firm ground rules. But it also is often a matter of peer pressure *among* parents, with those with weaker wills critical of—and angry at—those who hold the line. Why? Because bad parents will always resent good parents for making them look bad in front of other parents.

If her kid wants a tablet or unlimited texting privileges, a mom is likely to get the following messages from other moms: *What's the big deal?* And *Don't you want to be able to monitor them?* And *Aren't you worried that other kids are getting a leg up—that your kid is falling behind?*

But these devices are not benign. They can distort the way children see the world and can affect their behavior in ways we don't fully understand. Conscious parenting means being aware of that—and acting on that awareness.

So the first priority should be on setting limits. One to two hours on weekdays, not including for homework, and three hours per day on weekends is more than sufficient for even a high-schooler. I feel that *screen time* should be limited to one hour in grade school: We're talking computers, mobile phones, tablets, video games, television—all of it.

I'm not saying this limit setting is easy to do. The American Association of Pediatrics tried recommending specific limits and instead ended up with the vague term "reasonable." Why? Because it got so much pushback from parents who think that a limit of two hours a day is unreasonable—and many of these parents do not have the tools to control the actions of their kids. Attempting to limit screen time would only cause family strife.

> Cultivate a thick skin. If you have to be stricter than other parents, then so be it.

What I tell parents is *Hard as it is to do, you've got to protect your child's brain!* Because, neurologically, we really don't know the long-term impact of excessive use of electronics. And frankly, at this point, these devices are so pervasive that I don't even know if we could do an adequate study. About the only ones we could use as a control group would be Amish children.

But what we do know is that we're playing with our children's future and letting them be guinea pigs.

For instance, what impact will it have on their social skills moving ahead, or on their capacity for critical thinking, or on their speaking skills? It may be that a lot of the delayed speech we're seeing in young children today is the result of reduced face-to-face inter-action with adults. I know I'm seeing this more and more in the practice. Not long ago I had one little guy, a very charming 3-year-old, who is pretty much nonverbal. His parents said he spends a lot of time watching Nickelodeon and Nick Jr., so I observed him watching the Teletubbies, and he made these little squeak noises, as if communicating with the figures on the screen. It was remarkable—he could speak Teletubby, just not human speech.

You see a variation of that with older children—how they engage more with the characters on the tablet than with the human beings in their lives. And, of course, since the figures in artificial worlds of these games have been specifically designed to engage the children in that age group, the children don't have to stretch and grow as they interact with them the way they would if they were dealing with actual people in real life.

In short, we know enough to understand that we should be worried. Because it's not like we're going to be able to do a do-over with the development of our kid's brain.

If for that reason alone, we should be proactive. *We,* not our culture, should be the ones setting limits.

In any case, we have to build the foundation of our child's character first. The way to do that is as old as antiquity, and it doesn't involve electronic devices but rather interaction with the people who matter most in a child's life. So the fewer electronics, the better. We're working on a human being, and our task is not to be taken lightly. A parent has to think ahead.

And, of course, that goes at least as much for monitoring kids' social behavior as they get older—and, yes, taking the responsibility for it.

No question—sometimes parents have to cultivate a thick skin. I have a colleague who decided her daughter shouldn't go on a school trip that was a big celebratory event for the senior class. She and her husband were concerned about lack of supervision, teen drinking, sex—all the calamities that so often befall young people these days.

The result? Her phone started ringing off the hook with calls from other parents: *Why are you making your kid stay home from the trip? It's so mean! It's so unfair!* She and her husband tried to explain: "We're concerned that it is a situation that might be too much for her to handle. We'll celebrate on our own—and we'll celebrate as a family."

Like *that* was about to work! The other parents kept trying to talk them out of it—*shame* them out of their decision. Quite likely, some of them had the same concerns but weren't strong-willed enough to make an issue of it. Harsh as saying so sounds, having given into pressure from their kids—and other parents—they were ultimately more interested in defending themselves and their own choices than in protecting their kids.

But my friends held firm, and they were proven right. A number of the kids *did* get into real trouble on that trip.

> As a parent, sometimes you just have to love smarter than other parents.

A mom can never neglect her own voice. If she has to be stricter than other parents, so be it. It's her job to say, "We love you, but buying you stuff or letting you do whatever you want is not how we show it. Your friends are their own parents' responsibility. We're thinking long-term. We expect you're going to be fine, but you won't be fine if you make some horrible choice in high school that changes your life forever."

In short, a parent has to protect and train her child—not by taking opportunities away but by talking through situations and, if called for, by explaining to children why they are being raised differently from their friends. Fighting peer pressure is not for the here and now—you're looking down the road and making choices to give your child a better future.

The fact is, you look at the world through older, more experienced eyes. You see what your child cannot. Tell her: "Yes, I see that Matt is handsome. He's got a great smile, he's funny, and he was great in the school play. But *we* see a kid who has no parental supervision—who drives *twenty* miles an hour faster than the speed limit. And we don't want to pick you up out of a ditch."

Obviously, it's not always easy for the child, because there's enormous peer pressure from his or her end also. Your child will sometimes feel bad or feel left out. She is a kid, and kids want to be social and hang out with people. As the parent of a teenager, I understand that some of the lessons seem unreasonable in America today. "Don't be alone in a car with a boy any time you can help it" is a line no daughter wants to hear, let alone obey. But it's something as true as it ever was. Why? Because—and I'm only half-joking here—most boys are crazy until they turn 35 years old.

After a while, if a parent has done it right, the proper attitude is so embedded in a child that everyone sees it, including the other kids. They'll stop even asking him or her to join in going out at night or drinking, because asking is a waste of their time. As a parent, you sometimes just have to love smarter than other parents.

Protection is proactive. It's not turning away and hoping for the best. It is not behaving the wrong way just because other parents do. You're not saying *no* to be mean to 12-year-old Annie; you're saying *yes* to 35-year-old Annie, who's going to be real happy she didn't have a baby when she was 15 years old. Adult Annie will be grateful that her parents protected her.

The message cannot be repeated often enough: *I'm protecting you. I want you to go to college, and have amazing experiences. I want you to travel and experience life. If I don't do my job now, then you don't get to live your life later. So we're in this together.*

> If you don't do your job now, your child will have a harder life later.

Basically, you plant your flag, declaring *This is who we are; this is how we do it in our family.* You give your child an identity to hold onto, and you let him know he is not just part of the herd!

The bottom line is that there are many different paths through life, and the ones that pay off are not in the middle. They just aren't. When people try to parent down the middle, the result is middle kids: Parents get mush. These kids will turn out to be people who are most likely to just go along with the crowd.

Chapter Eighteen

BE THE PARENT YOU WANT YOUR CHILD TO BE

*T*o a certain degree, almost all of us are hypocrites, preaching what we do not practice, what we practice inconsistently, or what we practice only when all the stars are in alignment.

That's okay—it's called being human. At the same time, being a parent means being harder on ourselves, and more honest with ourselves, than we had to be when we were just looking out for number one. In short, you can't expect from your child what you don't expect of yourself. There are no perfect moments in parenting to do your job. There are only more moments to do your job.

With this in mind, I always advise parents to make a list of the flaws they see in themselves, then choose some to work on. A mom may spend too much time on the phone or watching television;

maybe she imbibes too much or doesn't listen as well as she should, or perhaps she too easily loses her temper. We're all sinners. But the point of this list is self-awareness. It acknowledges fault—and, by extension, is a challenge to improve that behavior. It is a reminder to be the best possible example for our children—a reminder and a *pledge*.

As parents, there is no more important promise we can make to ourselves than to model the person we're supposed to be. True, you may not feel like that person—at least not at the beginning—but think of it this way: If actors can convince you they're who they pretend to be, then we can roleplay also. And the funny thing is that the more we play that role, the more fully we become that person.

Of course, the things we are most hypocritical about can be the ones hardest to address. In an age when you walk into a restaurant and see every member of the family with head down, looking down at a device, how can a mom honestly tell her child to cut down on tablet use? And how can a mom who depends on the convenience of regular fast food dinners persuasively tell her kid to cut out junk food?

But have I said anywhere in this book that effective parenting is a snap? Think of it this way: If your child knows how hard it was for *you* to have changed your behavior, your modeling of that behavior is all the more effective.

The fact is, we teach maturity by example. This is another thing that was once generally understood but has been forgotten. Not so long ago, if a child's parents

> Don't expect of your child what you don't expect of yourself.

were farmers, their children understood how to farm. If they were engineers or construction workers, then their kids knew about that. Traditionally, that was part of the child's education and part of the modeling, so that even if they chose other lines of work, in key ways—in their values and work ethic and self-confidence—they would mirror their parents. It was part of the family legacy.

Few parents today understand this important fact; they'll value some extracurricular activity over something that child can learn only from them through hands-on experience. For example, I know a 16-year-old boy who is really floundering. His mom owns a successful store. Nothing would have done more for that boy's self-confidence than teaching him how to man the register, how to take care of the customers when they came in, and how to manage the money well, being responsible for it. If those things had occurred instead of his mom's signing him up for soccer and karate and busing him all over the place, he might be a more self-confident person—not where he is today.

But here's a happier outcome for a really nice young lady I know whose dad was an ENT doctor and whose mom was a nurse. When she was growing up, they would talk around the kitchen table about owning a practice and what different policies would do to their family business. She took that to heart, and although she knew she didn't want to be a doctor, she really felt very comfortable when it came to analyzing what changes in health care dictated by the government would do to their patients, their family, and their practice. As a result, now, in her mid-twenties, she's very successful as a health care analyst.

We've lost the understanding that education is more than just schooling. It's also what happens at home around the dinner table, in the car, and talking in the living room. I think of the Canadian fiddler Natalie MacMaster and what she's done for her children. She has five children, and two or three times a year, she includes them in her concerts. As a mom, it actually brings me to tears to see these kids and enjoy how wonderfully they perform, how full of life they are, and how proud they are of being on stage with their mom. It obviously took enormous persistence for her to teach these little tots how to do this so well.

Soon after their concert, I saw one of those children with her mom at a book signing, helping take the money from the customers and interacting with adults, and I was impressed even more. She was enthusiastic, poised, and learning.

So I was really taken aback when I told a colleague about this the next day, saying what a wonderful job this mom had done. Not only was she a phenomenal musician, but she was also passing that legacy on to her kids! The doctor to whom I was speaking looked scornful—outraged, even.

"What that mom is doing is forcing her values on her children!" she said. In fact, she thought it almost abusive.

My goodness! What a strange way of seeing things. These children were the opposite of abused: They were incredibly happy and self-confident. Had this mom *not* passed on some of what she had to her children, *that* would have been neglectful!

Far from forcing ourselves on our children, when we do things right, we're guiding them toward a better future.

How does anyone not see that? They don't because we're in this bizarre time when childhood is thought to be all about self-esteem. In fact, it is supposed to be preparing kids for adulthood. Children *want* to help; that's part of the way they learn. Have you ever seen with what excitement children dive into pretending to be a grocery store cashier, a police officer, or a waiter? And they take on these roles with enthusiasm and pride! They are still playing, and it's still exciting to them, but they're learning great skills at the same time.

My own mom worked for Lord and Taylor until I was 13 years old, and once a year, she'd take me to work. I was expected to sit there quietly, but if somebody asked me to do something, I was expected to answer politely and say, "Yes, I'll do that," and function as a little helper. Some of the nicest days I spent as a kid were going there. I'd get so excited at being allowed to dress up like my mom. We'd take the subway from Queens into Manhattan just like all the other men and women going to work. For one day each year, I got to pretend that I was an adult, and I learned to model myself after my mom.

Those are the kinds of experiences that we need to go back to sharing with our children again. These experiences help with the transition from school to adulthood and to the real world.

> Become self-aware. Acknowledge your flaws, and work to improve them.

Obviously, there is an age when a parent has to start letting go— when, having done his or her job properly, he has to trust that the child has gotten the message. Even when we're far away, years or even decades later, at key moments, our lessons will come back to our children.

Quite simply, when we parents show ourselves to our children in our work, in our lives, and in all our other dimensions, what we are modeling, finally, is *character*.

Indeed, sometimes the best lessons we teach are inadvertent.

That happened not long ago in my own household. Because I'd stood behind the North Carolina governor when he signed an anti–sanctuary city law, the progressive left targeted our practice. They made the rounds of the mobile home parks where some of our Hispanic parents live and went on radio shows saying I was a traitor to Hispanics, claiming I wanted them deported. We were getting threatening phone calls, and we needed police surveillance at our office. Never mind that I'd had the practice for 16 years, often not charging some of these same people when they couldn't afford to pay for treatment, praying with them, holding their hands; these activists used the instrument of fear to successfully spread their vicious lies. They told people that if they didn't abandon our practice, there would be repercussions. As a result, we lost more than 200 patients.

This was an awful thing to have happen—really heartbreaking. To me, these were not just patients and charts; they were lives I care about deeply.

There was one mom whose child's life I had literally saved at birth, when she went into labor at twenty-three-and-a-half weeks. At that time, I went out on a limb, taking on an older, respected OB/GYN to make sure the mother was transferred to a facility whose technology might help her baby survive. The baby was successfully delivered, and she grew up to be a normal child. I always relished seeing her, and when I saw her chart had been transferred to another practice, it just broke my heart. I called the mom, telling her how much I'd always cherished taking care of her daughter and letting her know how much I cared for her, warning her that the level of care at the other facility would not be close to the same. She would barely even answer.

But there was a huge saving grace. Hannah, who has been around the clinic since birth, and who knows it almost as well as I do, saw this—saw that her mom had stood on principle despite the costs. And from this, she learned lessons that will be with her the rest of her life.

> We teach maturity by example.

She has also seen all the good we have achieved, the stories of children who seemed lost but who have been retrieved—children like Peter, an 8-year-old boy who is autistic and developmentally delayed. His grandfather, a mechanic, takes care of him. When I first met Peter, he was an absolute mess—not all that different from Helen Keller before Annie Sullivan got hold of her. He couldn't speak, just screamed and yelled and couldn't even be examined because he'd jump up and down on the examining table. But we worked hard, both his grandfather and I. I told his grandfather that we keep nudging in the right direction, not letting ourselves be pushed backward by this young boy. "This is what a parent does," I said. "You nudge forward, and you never give an inch back."

That boy came in yesterday. He's polite, he's now potty-trained, and he puts his clothes on himself. He's starting to recognize three-letter words and sound them out—even converse a little. I was able to teach his grandfather the art of nudging so that he could do it for his grandson. So now, instead of this wild and uncontrollable being, we have a boy who can reach his God-given potential. We saved his life.

My daughter has seen all this—and so much more.

This is how children learn.

When moms decide to find their maternal voice, anything is possible. In 2014, I began seeing a teenage girl in my behavior clinic. She had been seen by our doctors for recurrent abdominal pain and had been skipping school. Mom was concerned because the daughter was dating boys that Mom did not approve of—behind Mom's back. This girl was at an age when she was the one who had to make a decision. I told her that she needed to submit herself to her mother's authority and that while she was under Mom's roof, she had to follow Mom's rules. More important, she needed to learn from her mother so that she would be prepared for life. Mom had to become the authority in the home and instruct her daughter rather than be her friend. Sally wanted to go on to college, but her grades were not good enough at that time. I told her that boys must come second if she wanted to become successful and to attain her dreams.

I saw Sally in clinic a short time ago. She is finishing her senior year of high school. She improved her grades and dumped the boys. She is now a proud and self-confident young woman. She was accepted into a private out-of-state four-year college, and she plans to become a teacher. She bubbled as she talked about her future and her plans: She would be the first in her family to go to college. I asked Mom if she thought that Sally was ready to go off into the world. The response that I got made what I do worthwhile. Mom said, "I've taught her everything that I could teach her. I'm ready to set her free."

After she left, I remembered how when I was 16, my mom sent me to Canada because she wanted me to learn French and had decided I was ready to live overseas without her. What an incredible moment it must have been for her to realize *Okay, my daughter is pretty close to being an adult. She's still going to be in somebody's home—and somebody's care—but I now trust that she is ready to act responsibly.*

> Show yourself to your children in all your dimensions.

She knew I'd internalized all the things she had taught me. She had prepared me not only for life but to *succeed* in life.

I remember, too, that around that time, people would single me out and say, even within my hearing, "She's heading somewhere"— and how great it felt to hear that. It wasn't *She's going to a great college* but *She's going somewhere.* And the "somewhere" was a bit intriguing, because although I didn't know exactly what it looked like, it was going to be a wonderful place. I was going somewhere—and off I went.

That's what we want for our kids: We want them to be that kid, headed somewhere.

I'll never forget how good it felt. It was exciting—my future was limitless! Yet I know it probably meant even more to my mom. It was actually she who had succeeded even more than I ever could. She had raised a successful adult and a good citizen for the next generation.

When we raise our kids with the goal of being the best person they can be, the person they are meant to become, we are ensuring a better future for everyone else's kids, too. Together, moms safeguard the future of our society, our culture, and our country. We do this for our kids first, and then—one child at a time—for us all! Only women get this, because it's a "mom thing."

EPILOGUE

*M*y family and I wanted the perfect final bullet point for this book. We spent hours tossing ideas back and forth: How could we sum up the final step in this important job of raising a child to be a good addition to society—letting him or her go?

Then I remembered that several months ago, I had the honor of sitting on the back porch of the home of the former secretary of education, Dr. William Bennett. It was a glorious Carolina afternoon at the beach, and the sun was warm on our backs. We recalled how when she was a little girl, Hannah and I would take turns reading his *Book of Virtues* before bedtime. Hannah told the former secretary of education how much she had enjoyed reading his books, and she described her favorite characters in great detail. After that, I asked Hannah to bring me something from the kitchen. She said, "Yes, ma'am" and went inside to do as asked.

As she walked away, Dr. Bennett looked over at her dad and me and remarked, "Your daughter has poise that exceeds her age. You must be doing a good job raising her. It is unusual to see this trait in our young people nowadays." (Yes, I remember every word!) Tears welled up in my eyes, and I was forced to turn away. I realized at that moment that my task of raising Hannah was nearly at an end. My turn in the circle of motherhood is ending, and someday my Hannah will take her turn at raising her own children to be good citizens. Few men can understand this heartwrenching moment in a mother's life, because "it's a mom thing."

Made in the USA
Columbia, SC
28 July 2021